Booth-Clibborn Editions

EUROPEAN ILLUSTRATION

1990 - 91

The seventeenth annual of
European editorial,
book, advertising,
poster, design, animated,
unpublished and
student illustration.

La dix-septième publication
annuelle d'illustrations
européennes pour
magazines et journaux,
livres, publicités, affiches,
design, enfin, illustrations
animées, oeuvres
non publiées, oeuvres
d'étudiants.

EDITOR
Edward Booth-Clibborn

ASSISTANT EDITOR
Jeremy Myerson

BOOK DESIGN
Lewis Moberly

ART DIRECTOR
Mary Lewis

DESIGNERS
Susanna Cucco
Nicky Perkins

COORDINATORS
Victoria Pratt
Beverley Parker

PHOTOGRAPHY
Alan David Tu

TRANSLATOR
Chantal Bordet

CONTENTS

CREDITS

**DIRECTEUR
DE LA REDACTION**
Edward Booth Clibborn

**ASSISTANT DIRECTEUR
DE LA REDACTION**
Jeremy Myerson

DESIGN DU LIVRE
Lewis Moberly

DIRECTEUR ARTISTIQUE
Mary Lewis

MISE EN PAGE
Susanna Cucco
Nicky Perkins

COORDINATEURS
Victoria Pratt
Beverley Parker

PHOTOGRAPHIE
Alan David Tu

TRADUCTRICE
Chantal Bordet

Booth-Clibborn Editions
ISBN 0 904866 84 X
Copyright 1990

European Illustration
Printed in Japon
by Dai Nippon

TABLE DES MATIERES

FOREWORD
BY EDWARD BOOTH-CLIBBORN

The past year has been an exciting one for EUROPEAN ILLUSTRATION. But for all that the stimulating prospect of opening our joint venture in Hull is obviously an on-going delight (see Jeremy Myerson's piece on page 9), what has thrilled me even more has been the wonderful response we've had to our Call for Entries from countries in the Eastern bloc. In the past this has been a mere trickle. This year it was a torrent.

Indeed, with more than two hundred artists submitting work from Russia, Poland, Rumania, Bulgaria, Yugoslavia, Hungary and Czechoslovakia, we could easily have considered changing our name to EAST EUROPEAN ILLUSTRATION! The result is a very different look to this year's annual.

Though some of the subject matter may seem grotesque to West European eyes, there is no denying the delightful quality in the drawings.

Apart from the sheer fascination in seeing so much work from these countries, it is more than simply satisfying to think that so many artists working in the Eastern bloc already perceive themselves as Europeans, sharing a common artistic heritage and a burgeoning political future.

To claim that EUROPEAN ILLUSTRATION has been responsible for this development alone would be outrageous. However, we may fairly claim to have set a trend in motion seventeen years ago, when we published our first annual, and to be sustaining its development through our project in Hull.

My hope is that we shall not falter: that Europe will continue to work towards the goal of creative co-operation, and that EUROPEAN ILLUSTRATION will continue to reflect all that's best in at least one aspect of our cultural and artistic life.

AVANT-PROPOS
PAR EDWARD BOOTH-CLIBBORN

L'année passée a été une année excitante pour EUROPEAN ILLUSTRATION. La perspective stimulante de l'ouverture de notre collaboration à Hull est évidemment un plaisir continu (se référer au texte de Jeremy Myerson, page 9); mais ce qui m'a fait vibrer plus encore, a été la réponse merveilleuse recue a notre appel d'entrées en provenance des pays de l'Est. Dans le passé ceci a ete un petit flot lent. Cette année c'était un torrent.

En effet avec plus de deux cents artistes soumettant leur travail, de Russie, Pologne, Roumanie, Bulgarie, Yougoslavie, Hongrie et Tchécoslovaquie, nous aurions aisément pu considérer changer notre nom pour EAST EUROPEAN ILLUSTRATION ! Le résultat est un look très différent pour cet annuel.

Bien que des sujets puissent paraitre grotesques aux yeux d'Europeens de l'Ouest, la qualité de certaines techniques employées est un delice indéniable. Le travail russe est particulièrement complexe, avec une qualité des dessins presque enchanteresse.

La douce fascination de voir tant de travail de ces pays mise à part, il est plus que satisfaisant de penser que tant d'artistes travaillant dans ces pays se percoivent déjà europeens, partageant un héritage artistique commun et un futur politique bourgeonnant.

Dire que EUROPEAN ILLUSTRATION a été seule responsable de ce développement serait abhérant. Quoiqu'il en soit, nous pouvons à juste titre prétendre avoir lancé une tendance, il y a dix-sept ans, en publiant notre premier annuel et en soutenant ce développement à travers notre projet à Hull.

Mon espoir maintenant, est que nous ne flaiblissions pas; que l'Europe continue à travailler vers la coopération créative et que EUROPEAN ILLUSTRATION reflète le meilleur dans au moins l'un des aspects de notre vie culturelle et artistique.

HULL: ILLUSTRATION'S GATEWAY TO EUROPE
BY JEREMY MYERSON

During the seventeen years that European Illustration has been in existence, the annual's publisher Edward Booth-Clibborn has been an avid personal collector of individual artworks. An enthusiast with an informed eye, Booth-Clibborn has bought the work of many young, rising and established illustrators.

Today his personal collection stands at more than 200 pieces, a body of work which provides a fascinating insight into the development of illustration during the past two decades.

But for a long time now, the question of how to store and display the collection has been a perplexing one for Edward Booth-Clibborn. It was last seen in its entirety at the Cooper Hewitt Museum in New York and the Pompidou Centre in Paris. But more recently it has been languishing neglected in boxes.

Now, however, a major initiative is set to bring this unique collection of European illustration permanently into the public domain. A new dockside museum facility in the city of Hull is set to open early in 1991, which will display all the artworks.

This magnificent enterprise is due to a unique collaboration between Edward Booth-Clibborn, who is donating his collection in its entirety, and a number of organisations in the public and private sector. They include Hull City Council, Lincolnshire and Humberside Arts Association, Humberside College of Higher Education and the developer Land Securities.

Why Hull? Edward Booth-Clibborn explains that the scheme came about via links he formed with the city when his son James went up to Hull University to read theology. During a visit to see his son, Booth-Clibborn was invited by Roger Bush, head of the school of art and design at Humberside College of Higher Education, to give a lecture.

Afterwards, in conversation, Booth-Clibborn confided his problem concerning his private collection of illustration and the idea of the European Illustration Trust was born. Roger Bush approached Lincolnshire and Humberside Arts, which was immediately interested in bringing an art collection of international significance to the region.

HULL: PORTE EUROPEENNE DE L'ILLUSTRATION
PAR JEREMY MYERSON

Depuis dix-sept ans qu'existe European Illustration, l'éditeur de l'annuel, Edward Booth-Clibborn, a été un collectionneur avide de maquettes individuelles. Enthousiaste à l'oeuil informé, Booth-Clibborn a achete le travail de nombreux jeunes, illustrateurs grimpants et confirmés.

Aujourd'hui sa collection personnelle s'élève a plus de 200 pièces, un corps de travail qui fournit un apercu fascinant du développement de l'illustration au cours de ces deux dernières décennies.

Mais depuis longtemps maintenant, pour Edward Booth-Clibborn, la question de comment ranger et presenter la collection s'est montrée complexe. Sa dernière présentation en intégralité a eu lieu au Cooper Hewitt Museum à New York et au Centre Pompidou à Paris. En revanche, plus récemment, elle a été languissante, négligée dans des boites.

Maintenant, quoiqu'il en soit, une initiative majeure a été établie pour apporter de facon permanente, cette unique collection d' illustration européenne, dans le domaine publique.

Un nouveau muséum sur les docks de la cité de Hull, s'apprête à ouvrir debut 1991, qui présentera toutes les maquettes.

Cette magnifique entreprise est due à une collaboration unique entre Edward Booth-Clibborn, qui a donné sa collection dans son intégralité et un nombre d'organisations des secteurs privé et publique. Ceux-ci incluent la municipalité de Hull, 'Lincolnshire et Humberside Arts Associations', 'Humberside College of Higher Education' et le promoteur 'Land Securities'.

Pourquoi Hull? Edward Booth-Clibborn explique que le projet est né par l'intermédiaire des liens qu'il a formé avec la ville, lorsque son fils James est monté à l'Université de Hull pour étudier la théologie. Lors d'une visite à son fils, Booth-Clibborn fut invité par Roger Bush, responsable de l'ecole d'art et design à 'Humberside College of Higher Education', pour donner un cours.

Plus tard, lors d'une conversation, Booth-Clibborn confia ses problèmes concernant sa collection privée d'illustrations et l'idée de l''European Illustration Trust' était née. Roger Bush approcha 'Lincolnshire et Humberside Arts', qui fut immédiatement intéressé pour apporter à la région une collection d'art de portée internationale.

According to the Arts Association's assistant director Alan Humberstone, who has responsibility for visual arts, 'There was a very positive reaction because everyone was excited at what would clearly be an artistic coup.'

A business plan was drawn up with the action focussed on the regeneration of Princes Dock in Hull. This is the site for a new shopping centre developed by Land Securities, which is being built on stilts across the dock and is set to open in November 1990.

At one end of the dock, the Ferens Art Gallery, Hull's principal art venue, is having a major new extension built (with much of the cost borne by Land Securities). At the other end of the dock there stands a Victorian warehouse – Warehouse 6. This has been earmarked to house Booth-Clibborn's collection on the ground floor. To complement the permanent collection there will be a bookshop, areas for study and other activities.

Edward Booth-Clibborn emphasises that he made two major stipulations in donating his collection: that it should be properly looked after and displayed; and that it should tour from its permanent base. Only work selected for publication in the European Illustration annuals is eligible for inclusion in the new museum.

The building's landlord, the City Council, has donated the venue and put in some pump-priming money to set the ball rolling. But the leader of Hull City Council, Patrick Doyle, emphasises that the success of the scheme depends on private sector sponsorship.

'We have got to raise in the region of £300,000,' he says. 'The project is extremely important to the city in the light of European developments in the run-up to 1992. Hull is taking on a more significant role as a Europort. We already have regular nightly sailings to and from Zebrugge and Rotterdam.'

The point about the European dimension of the new illustration museum is made by Lincolnshire and Humberside's Arts Director Clive Fox: 'It is of strategic importance to our plans to build up European cultural links. It also fits into the framework of making sure that the regeneration of the dockside is accompanied by cultural regeneration. There are certain similarities with Glasgow but on a different scale.'

Selon le directeur assistant de l''Arts Association', Alan Humberstone, qui a la responsabilité des art visuels, 'Il y avait une réaction très positive parceque chacun était excité à la perspective de ce qui serait clairement un coup artistique'

Un plan commercial a été tracé avec des actions concentrées sur la régénération de 'Princes Docks' à Hull. C'est le site d'un nouveau centre commercial développé par Land Securities, qui est construit sur pilotis à travers le dock et destiné à ouvrir en novembre 1990.

A une extrémiteé du dock, la 'Ferens Art Gallery', le principal centre artistique de Hull, fait construire une nouvelle extension majeure (avec une grande partie du coût supporté par Land Securities). A l'autre extremité du dock se trouve un entrepôt Victorien – Entrepot 6. Celui-ci a été marqué pour abriter au rez-de-chaussée la collection de Booth-Clibborn. Pour completer la collection permanente, il y aura une boutique de livres, des espaces pour l'étude et autres activités.

Edward Booth-Clibborn souligne qu'il a posé deux stipulations majeures en donnant sa collection: qu'elle soit soignée et présentée correctement et qu'elle voyage de sa base permanente. Seul le travail sélectionné pour la publication des annuels dans European Illustration est éligible pour l'inclusion dans le nouveau museum.

La propriétaire du batiment, la municipalité de la ville, a donné les lieux et injecté de l'argent pour lancer la balle. Mais le leader de 'Hull City Council', Patrick Doyle, souligne que le succès du projet dépend du sponsoring du secteur privé.

'Nous devons rassembler aux alentours de £300.000', dit-il. 'Le projet est extrèmement important pour la ville à la lumiere des développements européens et de la course vers 1992. Hull prend un rôle significatif en tant qu'Euro-port. Nous avons déjà des traversées de nuit régulières à destination et à partir de Zebrugge et Rotterdam.'

L'intérèt de la dimension europeenne du nouveau muséum d'illustration est relevé par le directeur de 'Lincolnshire et Humberside Arts', Clive Fox: 'Il est d'importance stratégique pour nos plans, de construire des liens culturels europeens. Il convient aussi au cadre de s'assurer que la régénération des docks s'accompagne d'une régénération culturelle. Il y a certaines similarités avec Glasgow, mais à une échelle différente.'

Fox adds: 'The Ferens Art Gallery extension will change an old-style civic gallery into one of national significance capable of housing big exhibitions. Opposite it, Warehouse 6, once restored, will set the architectural tone for the entire site.'

The warehouse designated for the illustration museum is the only original building left on the site. Garth Hall has been invited to design the building and Gert Dumbar to create the graphics.

Alan Humberstone says that once a couple of large sponsors commit to the scheme, other will swiftly follow. There is a palpable air of excitement about the project, not just in the city of Hull but in the creative art, advertising and design communities, which forsee the educational spin-offs of displaying such a large collection of printed illustration for the first time.

Naturally other 'commerce and culture' collaborations, many on waterfront sites, have paved the way for the Humberside venture. The Tate Gallery at Liverpool, the Design Museum in London Docklands and the Museum of Photography, Film and Television at Bradford have all signalled a trend.

But Hull is aiming for a flavour all its own. Council leader Patrick Doyle explains that in 1992 there will be a trade and culture festival in the city to celebrate the European single market – plus a commemoration of the 350th anniversary of the city's refusal to allow entry to Charles I in 1542. (This effectively triggered off the English Civil War).

Doyle sees the European Illustration museum as very much part of the city's spirit of 1992. 'We'll be working hard to make sure it happens,' he promises.

Fox ajoute: ' L'extension de la 'Ferens Art Gallery' transformera une gallerie civique ancien style en une gallerie d'importance nationale capable d'abriter de grandes expositions. Opposé à elle, l'entrepôt 6, une fois restauré, établiera le ton architectural pour le site entier.'

L'entrepôt désigné pour le museum d'illustration est l'unique batiment original restant sur le site. Garth Hall a été invité à dessiner le batiment et Gert Dumbar à creer les graphiques.

Alan Humberstone dit q'une fois l'engagement d'un couple de larges sponsors, d'autres suivront rapidement. L'air d'excitement relatif au projet est palpable, non seulement dans la cité de Hull, mais dans les communautés d'art créatif, publicité, design, qui prévoient des retombées pour l'éducation, consécutives à la présentation en première, d'une collection d'illustrations imprimées.

Naturellement d'autres collaborations 'Commerce et Culture', nombreuses sur les sites du bord de l'eau, ont pavé le chemin pour l'entreprise Humberside. La 'Tate Gallery' à Liverpool, le 'Design Museum' sur les docks de Londres et le muséum de la Photographie, 'Film et Television' à Bradford ont balisé la tendance.

Mais Hull s'oriente vers une saveur propre à elle seule. Le leader de la municipalité Patrick Doyle explique qu'en 1992, il y aura un festival de commerce et culture dans la ville pour célébrer le marché unitaire europeen, plus une commémoration du 350ème anniversaire d'un refus de la cité d'accorder son entrée à Charles 1er en 1542. (Ceci a effectivement amorcé la guerre civile Anglaise)

Doyle considère le museum d'illustration européenne comme partie de l'esprit 1992 de la cité. 'Nous allons travailler dur pour nous assurer que cela ait lieu,' promet-il.

THE JURY

JIM BUNKER

Jim Bunker began commissioning illustrators in the late 1960s as art director of Mayfair Magazine. He then became art director of The Connoisseur, the celebrated fine arts and antiques magazine, to which he introduced illustrated covers. In 1985 he joined leading British children's book publisher, Walker Books, and has since worked with some of the foremost picture book illustrators. His responsibilities include commissioning jacket illustration for Walker and Julia MacRae hardback fiction, as well as the design of theatrical publications and plays for Nick Hern Books.

ROBERT HENGEVELD

Robert Hengeveld was born in 1946 in Arnhem, Holland, where he studied in the graphic design department of the Academy of Art. In 1970 he started his career as a junior art director with a major advertising agency, but after two years he decided to work in publishing. He worked initially for a book publisher for five years, before moving into magazine publishing and working for VNU, the largest publishing company in the Netherlands. He subsequently spent more than ten years as a freelance art director, working for various magazines including Leef, Cosmopolitan and Blad. He is now art director of the Dutch edition of Elle.

ITALO LUPI

Italian designer and art director Italo Lupi has worked on the magazines Abitare, Shop, Zodiac and Progex, as well as designing exhibitions, museums and scenery for RAI television. With Achille Castiglioni he designed the general architectural layout for the International Exhibition of the XVII Milan Triennale. His awards include an Art Director Club of Milan first prize (1977) and a silver medal at the XIII International Graphics Biennale at Brno, Czechoslovakia (1988). Lupi is currently art director of Domus and Rivista IBM.

LE JURY

JIM BUNKER

Jim Bunker, en tant que directeur artistique de "Mayfair magazine", commenca à mendater des illustrateurs, à la fin des annees 60. Il devint ensuite directeur artistique de "The Connoisseur", le célèbre magazine des beaux-arts et antiquités, auquel il a introduit les couvertures illustrèes. En 1985 il s'est joint à l'éditeur britannique leader du livre d'enfants,Walker Books et a depuis travaillé avec ceux des illustrateurs pour livres, les plus en vue. Ses responsabilités incluent, commander des illustrations de couverture pour Walker et romans reliés de Julia MacRae, ainsi que le design des publications et pièces théatrales pour Nick Hern Books.

ROBERT HENGEVELD

Robert Hengeveld est né en 1946,à Arnhem, en Hollande, ou il a étudié dans le département design graphique de l'Académie d'Art. En 1970 il débuta sa carrière en tant que directeur artistique junior au sein d'une importante agence de publicité, mais deux ans plus tard il décida de se consacrer à l'imprimerie. Initialement il travailla pendant cinq ans pour un éditeur de livres, avant de quitter pour travailler dans l'édition de magazines, pour VNU, la compagnie d'édition la plus large aux Pays-Bas. Par la suite il a été plus de dix ans directeur artistique freelance, travaillant pour divers magazines incluant Leef, Cosmopolitan et Blad. Il est maintenant directeur artistique de l'édition hollandaise de Elle.

ITALO LUPI

Designer et directeur artistique italien, Italo Lupi a travaillé sur les magazines Abitare, Shop, Zodiac et Progex, ainsi que le design d'expositions, muséums et décors pour la Television Avec Achille Castiglioni il a dessiné la disposition architecturale générale pour l'exposition internationale de "Milan Triennale XVII". Ses distinctions incluent le premier prix (1977) de "Art Director Club of Milan" et une médaille d'argent à "International Graphics Biennale" de Brno, Tchécoslovaquie (1988). Lupi est maintenant directeur artistique de Domus et Rivista IBM.

PEDRO SILMON

Pedro Silmon was born in the UK in 1955, of mixed Spanish/English parentage. He studied graphic design at Newcastle Upon Tyne Polytechnic and the Royal College of Art, graduating in 1979. He immediately began working as a freelance designer for the Sunday Times, and became a staff member in 1982. He has been art director of the Sunday Times Magazine since July 1985, and is responsible for commissioning most of the illustration work which appears in the Magazine. His design work has appeared most notably in Design and Art Direction and the Warsaw Poster Biennale, and his commissioned illustration and photography work has been widely recognised in exhibitions and publications. His book The Bikini, which he edited and designed, was published by Virgin Books in 1986.

LYNN TRICKETT

Graphic designer Lynn Trickett studied at Chelsea School of art and then worked in London and New York before setting up Trickett and Webb in 1971 with Brian Webb. Since then , Trickett and Webb have collaborated with imaginative clients (and some of the best illustrators) to produce award-winning work – "providing pleasure and profit for all concerned".

PEDRO SILMON

Pedro Silmon est né au Royaume-Uni en 1955, de parenté mixteEspagnole/Anglaise. Il a etudié le design graphique à la polytechnique de Newcastle Upon Tyne et au "Royal College of Art"; il est diplômé en 1979. Il a immédiatement commencé à travailler en tant que designer freelance pour le Sunday Times, est devenu employé en 1982. Il est directeur artistique du Sunday Times Magazine depuis juillet 1985 et responsable de la commission de la plupart des travaux d'illustration qui apparaissent dans le magazine. Son travail en matière de design est apparu notemmant dans "Design and Art Direction" et "Warsaw Poster Biennale" et son mendat de travaux d'illustration et photographie a été largement reconnu dans des expositions et publications. Son livre "The Bikini", qu'il a dessiné et rédigé, a été publié par Virgin Books en 1986.

LYNN TRICKETT

Designer graphique Lynn Trickett a étudié à "Chelsea School of Art", puis travaillé à Londres et New York avant de former Trickett & Webb en 1971 avec Brian Webb. Depuis lors, Trickett & Webb ont collaboré avec des clients imaginatifs (et ceux des meilleurs illustrateurs) pour produire des oeuvres distinguées de prix - "Offrir plaisir et profit a tous ceux concernés".

EDITORIAL

JOURNAUX, MAGAZINES

PAOLA PIGLIA

'Fehlt der Schliff, Knirshen die Kufen'. Illustration for an article about iceskating.
Acrylic.

'Fehlt der Schliff, knirshen die Kufen'. Illustration pour un article sur le Patin à glace.
Acrylique.

Designer / *Maquettiste:* Hans-Georg Pospischil

Publisher / *Éditeur:* Frankfurter Allgemeine Zeitung

PAOLA PIGLIA

'The Happy Couple'. Illustration for an article about pelicans.
Acrylic.

'L'Heureux Couple'. Illustration pour un article sur les pélicans.
Acrylique.

Designer / *Maquettiste:* Hans-Georg Pospischil

Publisher / *Éditeur:* Frankfurter Allgemeine Zeitung

PAOLA PIGLIA

'The Scribes'. Illustration for an article about pelicans.
Acrylic.

'Les Scribes'. *Illustration pour un article sur les pélicans.*
Acrylique.

Designer / *Maquettiste:* Hans-Georg Pospischil

Publisher / *Éditeur:* Frankfurter Allgemeine Zeitung

TOBY MORRISON

'Special Report: Urban Renewal'. Business Magazine illustration showing varying aspects of urban renewal.
Monoprint, fingerprint, paint and pencil.

*'Rapport Spécial: le Renouveau Urbain'. Illustration dans le magazine 'Business' montrant les
aspects variés du renouveau urbain.
Mono-imprimerie, imprimerie aux doigts, peinture et crayon.*

Designer / *Maquettiste:* Jim McClure

Publisher / *Éditeur:* Conde Nast Publications

TOBY MORRISON

'Special Report: Urban Renewal'. Business Magazine illustration showing varying aspects of urban renewal.
Monoprint, fingerprint, paint and pencil.

'Rapport Spécial: le Renouveau Urbain'. *Illustration dans le magazine 'Business' montrant les*
aspects variés du renouveau urbain.
Mono-imprimerie, imprimerie aux doigts, peinture et crayon.

Designer / *Maquettiste:* Jim McClure

Publisher / *Éditeur:* Conde Nast Publications

DAVID HUGHES

'Jack the Lad'. Caricature of actor Jack Nicholson for Observer magazine cover.
Mixed media.

'Jack le Gamin'. *Caricature de l'acteur Jack Nicholson pour une couverture de l''Observer Magazine'.*
Techniques diverses.

Designer / *Maquettiste:* David Hughes

Publisher / *Éditeur:* The Observer

BRIAN CRONIN

'**Peace**'. Rolling Stone Magazine illustration for the Second Essay on Peace.
Pen, ink and watercolour.

'*Paix*'. *Illustration dans le Magazine 'Rolling Stone', pour le Second Essai sur la Paix.*
Plume, encre et aquarelle.

Designer / *Maquettiste:* Fred Woodward

Publisher / *Éditeur:* Rolling Stone

BRIAN CRONIN

"Peace". Rolling Stone Magazine illustration for the First Essay on Peace.
Pen, ink and watercolour.

"Paix". *Illustration dans le magazine 'Rolling Stone', pour le premier Essai sur la Paix.*
Plume, encre et aquarelle.

Designer / *Maquettiste:* Fred Woodward

Publisher / *Éditeur:* Rolling Stone

BRIAN CRONIN

'Peace'. Rolling Stone Magazine illustration for the Third Essay on Peace.
Pen, ink and watercolour.

'Paix'. *Illustration dans le magazine 'Rolling Stones', pour le Troisième Essai sur la Paix.*
Plume, encre et aquarelle.

Designer / *Maquettiste:* Fred Woodward

Publisher / *Éditeur:* Rolling Stone

BRIAN CRONIN

'**The Triumph of the Individual**'. Sourcebook Magazine illustration.
Ink and watercolour.

'***Le Triumph de l'Individu***'. *Illustration pour le magazine 'Sourcebook'.*
Encre et aquarelle.

Designer / *Maquettiste:* Richard Bates

Publisher / *Éditeur:* Whittle Communications

BRIAN CRONIN

'**Zeit die Neue Wahrung**'. Illustration for an article about the madness of modern life.
Pen, ink and watercolour.

'***Zeit die neue Wahrung***'. Illustration pour un article sur le thème 'La Folie de la vie moderne'.
Plume, encre et aquarelle.

Designer / *Maquettiste:* Alan Foreman / Sylvia Geier

Publisher / *Éditeur:* Manner Vogue

CATHERINE DENVIR

'The new Modesty'. Tempo Magazine illustration.
Collage and watercolour.

'La nouvelle Modestie'. *Illustration pour le magazine 'Tempo'.*
Aquarelle et collage.

Designer / *Maquettiste:* Astrid Proll

Publisher / *Éditeur:* Tempo

ALAN YOUNG

'**Once upon a Time**'. Esquire Magazine illustration for a short story about apartheid.
Watercolour.

'*Il était une Fois*'. *Illustration pour le magazine 'Esquire', pour une nouvelle sur l'apartheid.*
Aquarelle.

Designer / *Maquettiste:* Wolfgang During

Publisher / *Éditeur:* Heinrich Bauer Spezialzeitschriftenverlag

CLAUDIO MUNOZ

'The Influence of Coincidence and Fate in Life'. Observer Magazine illustration.
Pen, ink and water-colour.

'L'Influence de la Coincidence et du Destin dans la Vie'.
Illustration pour l''Observer Magazine'.
Plume, encre et aquarelle.

Designer / *Maquettiste:* Graham Mitchener

Publisher / *Éditeur:* Observer Magazine

CLAUDIO MUNOZ

'Differences between Canadians and Americans'. Observer Magazine illustration.
Pen, ink and watercolour.

'Différences entre Americains et Canadiens'. Illustration pour l''Observer Magazine'.
Plume, encre et aquarelle.

Designer / *Maquettiste :* Graham Mitchener

Publisher / *Éditeur:* Observer Magazine

JAMEL AKIB

'Mail order in America'. Observer Magazine illustration.
Chalk and pastel.

'Commande par correspondance en Amerique'. Illustration pour l''Observer Magazine'.
Craie et pastel.

Designer / *Maquettiste:* Jo Plent

Publisher / *Éditeur:* Observer Magazine

ANDREW BYLO

'Preparing Lunch'. Day in the life of a Grand Hotel.
Watercolour and gouache.

'Préparer le déjeuner'. *Une journée passée dans un Grand Hotel.*
Aquarelle et gouache.

Designer / *Maquettiste:* Jim Brewster

Publisher / *Éditeur:* Reed Publishing

PENELOPE SOBR

'Fashion forecast for hosiery'. Illustrations about the new look of the season.
Gouache.

'Prévision de mode pour les bas et collants'. Illustrations présentant le nouveau look de la saison.
Gouache.

Designer / *Maquettiste:* Robby Laughton

Publisher / *Éditeur:* Caroline Neville Associates

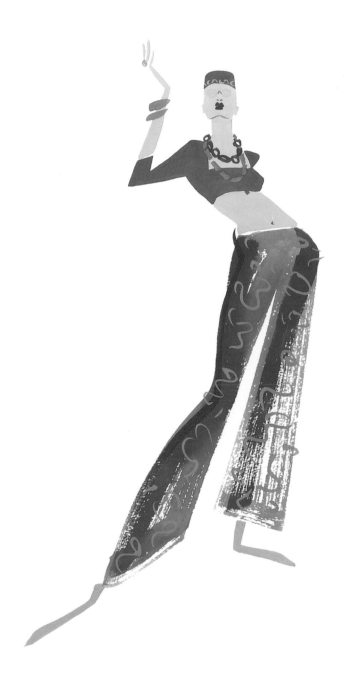

PENELOPE SOBR

'Fashion forecast for hosiery'. Illustration about the new look of the season.
Gouache.

'Prévision de mode pour les bas et collants'. Illustration présentant le nouveau look de la saison.
Gouache.

Designer / *Maquettiste:* Robby Laughton

Publisher / *Éditeur:* Caroline Neville Associates

PAUL SLATER

'Life on a Plate'. Sunday Times Magazine illustration.
Acrylic.

'La vie sur un Plateau'. Illustration pour le magazine 'Sunday Times'.
Acrylique.

Designer / *Maquettiste:* Pedro Silmon

Publisher / *Éditeur:* News International

PAUL LEITH

'Courage to Care'. Conneticut's Finest illustration for an article about children with AIDS.
Acrylic.

'Le Courage de se préoccuper'. *Illustration dans le magazine 'Conneticut's Finest' pour un article
sur les enfants avec le SIDA.*
Acrylique.

Art Director / *Directeur Artistique:* Laurence Woodhull

Publisher / *Éditeur:* Whittle Communications

IAN POLLOCK

'Luciano Pavarotti'. Sunday Times Magazine illustration for Critics Choice.
Watercolour, ink and gouache.

*'Luciano Pavarotti'. Illustration dans le 'Sunday Times Magazine' pour le Choix des Critiques.
Aquarelle, encre et gouache.*

Designer / *Maquettiste:* Pedro Silmon

Publisher / *Éditeur:* News International

IAN POLLOCK

'Buddy, can you spare a video link?'. Observer Magazine illustration showing how American politicians dwarf their English counterparts.
Watercolour, ink and gouache.

'Buddy, peux-tu réserver un canal video?'. *Illustration dans l''Observer Magazine', montrant comment les politiciens Américains écrasent leurs homologues anglais.
Aquarelle, encre et gouache .*

Designer / *Maquettiste:* Graham Mitchener

Publisher / *Éditeur:* Observer Magazine

IAN POLLOCK

'His Master's Vice'. Sunday Times Magazine illustration for an article on owners
allowing their dogs to foul pavements.
Watercolour, ink and gouache.

'Le Vice de son Maître'. Illustration dans le 'Sunday Times Magazine', pour un article sur les
propriétaires permettant à leurs chiens de salir les trottoirs.
Aquarelle, encre et gouache.

Designer / *Maquettiste:* Pedro Silmon

Publisher / *Éditeur:* News International

STANISLAS BOUVIER

'Ci-giesberd qui passa l'âme à droite'. Rolling Stone Magazine illustration.
Oil paint on paper.

'Ci-giesberd qui passa l'âme à droite'. *Illustration pour le magazine 'Rolling Stone'.*
Peinture à l'huile sur papier.

Publisher / *Éditeur:* Rolling Stone

STANISLAS BOUVIER

'Tout pour le Fric'. Rolling Stone Magazine illustration.
Oil paint on paper.

'Tout pour le Fric'. *Illustration pour le magazine 'Rolling Stone'.*
Peinture à l' huile sur papier.

Publisher / *Éditeur:* Rolling Stone

STANISLAS BOUVIER

'Qui censure quoi?'. Cosmopolitan Magazine illustration.
Oil paint on paper.

'Qui censure quoi?'. *Illustration pour le magazine 'Cosmopolitan'.*
Peinture à l'huile sur papier.

Publisher / *Éditeur:* Cosmopolitan

JOHN MORRIS

'Nuclear Balance'. CND Magazine illustration for an article linking poverty in Britain and the campaign against nuclear weapons.
Mixed media.

'Equilibre Nucléaire'. *Illustration dans 'CND Magazine' pour un article liant la pauvreté en Angleterre à la campagne contre l'armement nucléaire.*
Techniques diverses.

Designer / *Maquettiste:* Peter Cole

Publisher / *Éditeur:* CND Publications

MIKEY GEORGESON

'Flexible Friends'. New Statesman & Society Magazine illustration for an article showing the changing face of social sciences in the 1990's.
Linocut

'Amis Flexibles'. *Illustration dans le magazine 'New Statesman & Society', pour un article montrant le visage changeant des sciences sociales dans les années 90.*
Linogravure

Designer / *Maquettiste:* Caroline Heler

Publisher / *Éditeur:* New Statesman & Society

DOVRAT BEN-NAHUM

'Formula Wonders'. Illustrations for Harpers & Queen Magazine article about racing cars.
Mixed media.

'Formule Miracle'. *Illustrations dans le magazine 'Harpers & Queen', pour un article sur les voitures de course.*
Techniques diverses.

Designer / *Maquettiste:* Lawrence Morton

Publisher / *Éditeur:* Conde Nast Publications

JANET WOOLLEY

'Lyle Lovett'. Portrait of the Singer for Campus Voice.
Acrylic.

'Lyle lovett'. *Portrait du Chanteur pour 'Campus Voice'.*
Acrylique.

Designer / *Maquettiste:* Jennifer Jessee

Publisher / *Éditeur:* Whittle Communications

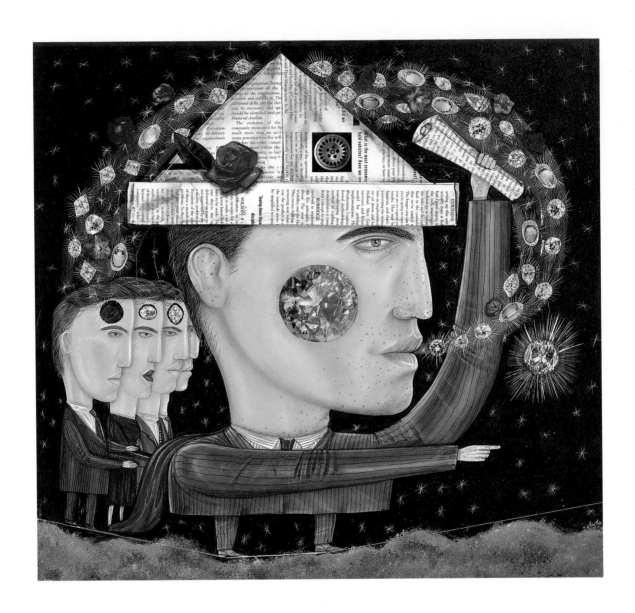

JANET WOOLLEY

'Leaders and managers'. Expo Magazine illustration.
Acrylic paint collage.

'Leaders et managers'. *Illustration pour 'Expo Magazine'.*
Collage peinture acrylique.

Art Director/*Directrice artistique*: Sue Wells

Publisher / *Éditeur:* Expo Magazine

JANET WOOLLEY

'Taking Action Against AIDS'. Illustration in Campus Voice for an article about AIDS.
Acrylic.

'Passer a l'action contre le SIDA'. *Illustration dans 'Campus Voice', pour un article sur le thème du SIDA.*
Acrylique.

Designer / *Maquettiste:* Jennifer Jessee

Publisher / *Éditeur:* Whittle Communications

ANNA OSTROWSKA

'Capricorn'. Horoscope illustration for Elle Magazine.
Acrylic.

'Capricorne'. *Illustration d'horoscope pour le magazine 'Elle'.*
Acrylique.

Designer / *Maquettiste:* Robert Hengeveld

Publisher / *Éditeur:* Hachette / VBD Magazines V.B.

ANNA OSTROWSKA

'Aquarius'. Horoscope illustration for Elle Magazine.
Acrylic.

'Verseaux'. *Illustration d'horoscope pour le magazine 'Elle'.*
Acrylique.

Designer / *Maquettiste:* Robert Hengeveld

Publisher / *Éditeur:* Hachette / VBD Magazines V.B.

JEREMY NORTON

'Only Connect'. Cover for Practical Computing Magazine.
Computer generated image.

*'**Connectez Seulement**'. Couverture du magazine 'Practical Computing'.
Image concue sur ordinateur.*

Publisher / *Éditeur:* Reed Business Publishing

PETER GRUNDY

Cover and illustration for 'Reuter Allert', Reuter's quarterly newsletter.
Separated art work.

Couverture et illustration pour 'Reuter Allert', *le journal trimestriel de la compagnie 'Reuter'.*
Maquette separée.

Designer / *Maquettiste:* Karen Blincoe

Publisher / *Éditeur:* Reuter Limited

JEAN-CHRISTIAN KNAFF

'Japanese Wisdom gets Electric'. Best of Business International magazine illustration.
Watercolour and mixed media.

'La Sagesse japonnaise devient Electrique'. *Illustration pour le magazine 'Best of Business International'.*
Aquarelle et techniques diverses.

Designer / *Maquettiste:* Bett McLean

Publisher / *Éditeur:* Whittle Communications

JEAN-CHRISTIAN KNAFF

'**Gemini** '. Horoscope illustration for Marie-Claire.
Watercolour and mixed media.

'**Gémeaux**'. *Illustration d'horoscope pour 'Marie-Claire'.*
Aquarelle et techniques diverses.

Designer / *Maquettiste:* Bernard Aldabe

Publisher / *Éditeur:* Marie-Claire - Paris

STUART BRIERS

'Reuter Position - Keeping Service'. Reuter Alert Magazine illustration of new links between products.
Gouache.

*'La Position de Reuter, guardant le Service'. Illustration des nouveaux liens entre produits,
pour le magazine 'Reuter Alert'. .
Gouache.*

Designer / *Maquettiste:* Karen Blincoe

Publisher / *Éditeur:* Reuter Limited

PETER TILL

'How sick are the British: how would you describe your weight?' . Observer Magazine illustration.
Pen, ink and watercolour.

'Dans quelle mesure les Britanniques sont-ils malades: comment décririez vous votre poids?'.
Illustration pour l''Observer Magazine'.
Plume, encre et aquarelle.

Designer / *Maquettiste:* Graham Mitchener

Publisher / *Éditeur:* Oserver Magazine

PETER TILL

'Scribes and Fallacies'. Observer Magazine illustration for an article about sending letters of complaint to editors.
Pen, ink, watercolour and coloured pencil.

'Scribes et Erreurs'. *Illustration dans l'*'Observer Magazine', *pour un article sur le thème 'Envoyer des lettres de doléances aux rédacteurs en chef'.*
Plume, encre aquarelle et crayons de couleur.

Designer / *Maquettiste:* Graham Mitchener

Publisher / *Éditeur:* Observer Magazine

PETER TILL

'How sick are the British: do you take tranquilisers?'. Observer Magazine illustration.
Pen, ink and watercolour.

'Dans quelle mesure les Britanniques sont-ils malades: prenez vous des tranquillisants?'.
Illustration pour l''Observer Magazine'.
Plume, encre et aquarelle.

Designer / _Maquettiste:_ Graham Mitchener

Publisher / _Éditeur:_ Observer Magazine

PETER TILL

'How sick are the British?'. Observer Magazine illustration for an opinion poll on the nations' health.
Pen, ink and watercolour.

'Dans quelle mesure les Britanniques sont-ils malades?'. Illustration dans l''Obsever Magazine'
pour un sondage sur la santé nationale.
Plume, encre et aquarelle.

Designer / *Maquettiste:* Graham Mitchener

Publisher / *Éditeur:* Observer Magazine

PETER TILL

'Barking Mad?'. Illustration in Country Living Magazine, for an article about people and their dogs.
Pen, ink and watercolour.

'Aboyer Stupide?'. *Illustration dans 'Country Living Magazine', pour un article sur les gens et leurs chiens.*
Plume, encre et aquarelle.

Designer / *Maquettiste:* Nick Dixon

Publisher / *Éditeur:* National Magazine Co

RHONALD BLOMMESTIJN

'Graduated'. Playboy Magazine illustration. A graduate looks back on his unhappy life as a student.
Oil on photograph.

'Diplôme'. Illustration pour 'Playboy'. Un diplômé se penche en arrière vers sa vie malheureuse d'étudiant.
Huile sur photographie.

Designer / *Maquettiste:* Piet Van Oss

Publisher / *Éditeur:* Playboy Nederland

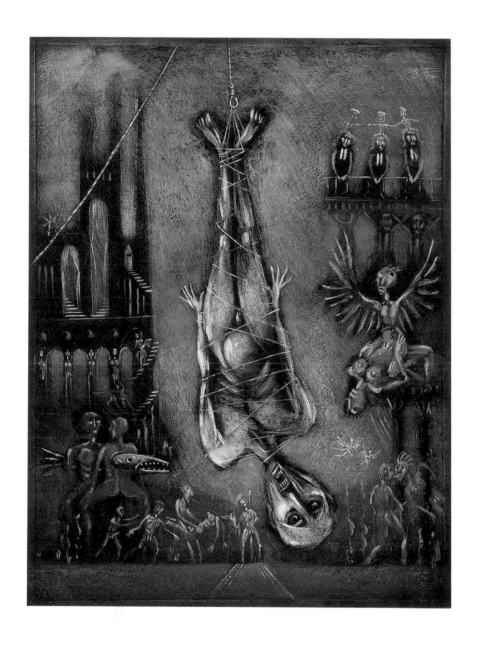

RICHARD PARENT

'Cry of Rape'. G.Q. Magazine illustration.
Acrylic and oil pastel

'Cri du Viol'. Illustration pour 'G.Q. Magazine'.
Acrylique et pastel a l'huile.

Designer / *Maquettiste:* Richard Parent

Publisher / *Éditeur:* G.Q. Magazine

GEOFFREY GRANDFIELD

'After Post-Modernism'. Blueprint Magazine illustration.
Chalk and pastel.

'Après le Post-Modernisme'. *Illustration pour le magazine 'Blueprint'.*
Craie et pastel.

Publisher / *Éditeur:* Blueprint Magazine

YAN NASCIMBENE

'Le Revenu Francais' Magazine illustration pointing out the rare value of estate stock investment.
Ink, watercolour and colour pencils.

Illustration pour 'Le Revenu Francais', *montrant la valeur rare de l'investissement immobilier.*
Encre, aquarelle, crayons de couleur.

Designer / *Maquettiste:* Yan Nascimbene

Publisher / *Éditeur:* Le Revenu Francais

ANDRZEJ DUDZINSKI

'**In the Air**'. Travel & Leisure Magazine illustration.
Oil crayon and pastel on paper.

'***Dans l'Air***'. *Illustration pour le magazine 'Travel & Leisure'.*
Crayon a l'huile et pastel sur papier.

Designer / *Maquettiste:* Daniela Wanda Maioresco

Publisher / *Éditeur:* American Express Editions

ANDRZEJ DUDZINSKI

'Money 2000'. Reuter Alert Magazine cover on the speed and flexibility of a major new product.
Pastels.

'Argent 2000'. *Couverture du magazine 'Reuter Alert', sur la rapidité et la flexibilité d'un produit nouveau majeur.*
Pastels.

Designer / *Maquettiste:* Karen Blincoe

Publisher / *Éditeur:* Reuter Limited

BART GOLDMAN

'The fast Art of Merging'. Best of Business International magazine illustration.
Oil paint.

*'L'Art rapide de Fusionner'. Illustration pour le magazine 'Best of Business International'.
Peinture a l'huile.*

Designer / *Maquettiste:* Bett McLean

Publisher / *Éditeur:* Whittle Communications

ANDREW MOCKETT

'Soaps and Self Censorship '. Illustration showing the Emergence of Hungarian TV from the Russian Communist Stranglehold.
Woodcut.

'Savons et Auto-Censure'. *Illustration montrant l'Émergeance de la Télévision Hongroise face à l'Étreinte Communiste Russe.*
Gravure sur bois.

Designer / *Maquettiste:* Seonaid Mackenzie

Publisher / *Éditeur:* Forward Publishing

CAROLYN GOWDY

'Living in Gin'. G.Q. Magazine illustration for an article about gin, as the consoling beverage
of widows, wrecks and wretches .
Mixed media.

'Vivre dans le Gin'. *Illustration dans 'G.Q. Magazine', pour un article sur le thème du gin, la boisson
réconfortante des veuves, des épaves et des pauvres diables.
Techniques diverses.*

Designer / *Maquettiste:* Margaret Donegan

Publisher / *Éditeur:* Conde Nast Publications

For your design needs

CAROLYN GOWDY

'Council Premises'. Graphics World Magazine illustration for an article about former 'Design Centre Shop'.
Mixed media.

*'Les Locaux du Design Council'. Illustration dans 'Graphics World Magazine', pour un article sur
l' ex-boutique du 'Design Centre'.
Techniques diverses.*

Designer / *Maquettiste:* Colin Sands

Publisher / *Éditeur:* Graphics World Magazine

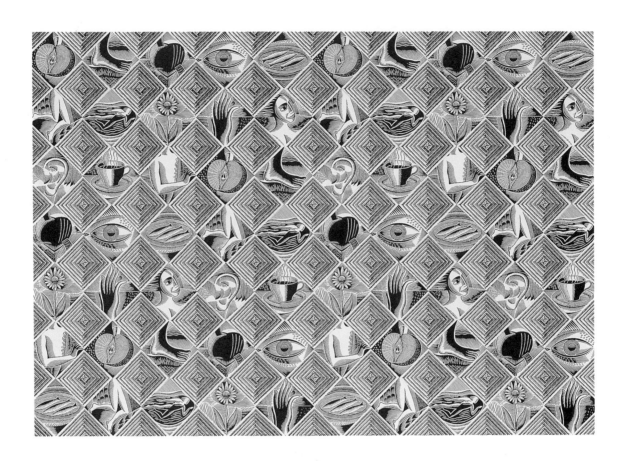

CLIFFORD HARPER

'Preventive Medicine'. Illustrated covers for a series of information booklets on preventive medicine.
Commissionned by the Sunday Times Magazine.
Ink.

'Médecine préventive'. *Couvertures illustrées pour une serie de brochures sur la médecine préventive.*
Commandées par le 'Sunday Times Magazine'.
Encre.

Designer / *Maquettiste:* Ian Bulloch

Publisher / *Éditeur:* News International

HELEN J. HOLROYD

'Ladled with Love (Gazpacho)'. Elle Magazine illustration.
Collage.

'Servi avec Amour (Gazpacho)'. *Illustration pour le magazine 'Elle'.*
Collage.

Designer / *Maquettiste:* Gavin Shaw

Publisher / *Éditeur:* News International-Hachette

ANNE HOWESON

'Leak Soup'. Illustration for article in G.Q. Magazine/New York,
about gossip and rumours in office life.
Gouache.

'Soupe au poireau'. *Illustration dans 'G.Q. Magazine'/New York, pour un article
sur les commères et rumeurs dans la vie de bureau.*
Gouache.

Designer / *Maquettiste:* Robert Priest

Publisher / *Éditeur:* G.Q. Magazine New York

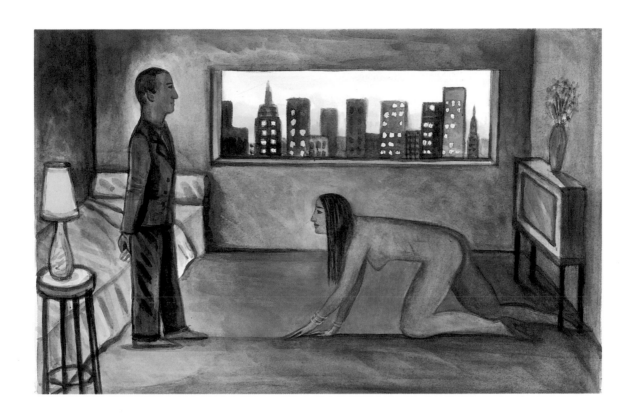

ANNE HOWESON

'Chicago Loop'. Illustration for an extract from a novel by Paul Theroux.
Gouache and watercolour.

*'Chicago Loop'. Illustration pour l'extrait d'un roman de Paul Theroux.
Gouache et aquarelle.*

Commissionning Editor / *Directrice de l'édition:* Deirdre Rooney

Publisher / *Éditeur:* Harpers & Queen Magazine

PIERRE-NOEL BERNARD

'Illustration on the theme "The Book"'. for the magazine 'Lire', heading the section 'Games'.
Mixed media.

'Illustration sur le thème du livre'. *en ouverture de la rubrique 'Jeux' du magazine 'Lire'.*
Techniques diverses.

Art director / *Directeur artistique:* Jean-Pierre Cliquet

Publisher / *Éditeur:* Lire

ALLAN DRUMMOND

'Choosing and Using Paper'. Design Magazine cover.
Gouache and pencil.

'Choisir et Utiliser le Papier'. *Couverture de 'Design Magazine'.*
Gouache et crayon.

Designer / *Maquettiste:* Polly Kerrs

Publisher / *Éditeur:* The Design Council

RAY NICKLIN

'Whose Car is it Anyway?'. Director Drive Magazine illustration about employee's liability
when driving a company car.
Pastel.

'De toute façon, à qui est cette Voiture?'. *Illustration dans le magazine 'Director Drive', sur la
responsabilité de l'employé au volant d'un véhicule de l'entreprise.*
Pastel.

Designer / *Maquettiste:* David Eachus

Publisher / *Éditeur:* The Director Publications Limited

MICHAEL SHEEHY

'The Green Issue'. Marketing Magazine illustration about the contrast between the 80's consumerism
and the more caring attitude in the 90's.
Mixed media.

'L'Issue Verte'. *Illustration dans le magazine 'Marketing', sur le thème du contraste entre le consumerisme des
années 80 et l'attitude bienveillante de la décennie 90.*
Techniques diverses.

Designer / *Maquettiste:* Mark Porter

Publisher / *Éditeur:* Haymarket Publications Limited

WALTER VAN LOTRINGEN

'How Macho is the Swiss Male?'. Illustration for an article about Swiss men.
Acrylic.

'Dans quelle mesure le Male Suisse est-il Macho ?'. Illustration pour un article sur le thème des hommes Suisses.
Acrylique.

Designer / *Maquettiste:* Kamwah Chan

Publisher / *Éditeur:* Tages Anzeiger Ag Zurich

WALTER VAN LOTRINGEN

'Ceci n'est pas un Chapeau'. Illustration on the renewed interest in wearing hats.
Acrylic.

'Ceci n'est pas un Chapeau' Illustration sur le renouveau d'intérêt à l'égard du port de chapeaux.
Acrylique.

Designer / *Maquettiste:* Walter Van Lotringen

Publisher / *Éditeur:* Uitgeuery Spaarwestad

JEFF FISHER

'Recycling'. New Scientist Magazine cover, on the theme 'Lizards losing their tails'.
Acrylic.

'Recycler'. *Couverture du magazine 'New Scientist', sur le thème des 'Lezards perdant leur queue'.*
Acrylique.

Designer / *Maquettiste:* Chris Jones

Publisher / *Éditeur:* IPC Magazines

JEFF FISHER

'Summer Bait'. Observer Magazine cover. Illustration launching a season of short stories.
Ink and watercolour.

*'Amorce d'Ete'. Couverture de l''Observer Magazine'. Illustration inaugurant une saison de nouvelles.
Encre et aquarelle.*

Designer / *Maquettiste:* Simon Esterson

Publisher / *Éditeur:* Observer Magazine

JEFF FISHER

'Bugs Abroad'. Business Magazine illustration for an article about health risks of travelling.
Acrylic.

'Germes à l'Etranger'. *Illustration dans le magazine 'Business', pour un article sur les risques sanitaires du voyage.*
Acrylique.

Designer / *Maquettiste:* Debra Zuckerman

Publisher / *Éditeur:* Conde Nast Publications

JEFF FISHER

'Edinburgh Festival'. Observer Magazine cover for a special edition.
Ink, watercolour, acrylic.

'Le Festival d'Edinburgh'. Couverture de l''Observer Magazine' pour une édition spéciale.
Encre, aquarelle, acrylique.

Designer / *Maquettistes:* Dave Ashmore & Steven Stafford

Publisher / *Éditeur:* Observer Magazine

DAVID WEBSTER

'Business Education for Designers'. Design Magazine illustration for an article about new
business courses for designers.
Ink and watercolour.

'Enseignement Commerciale pour Designers' *Illustration pour 'Design Magazine', destinée à un
article sur de nouveaux Cours Commerciaux pour designer.
Encre et aquarelle.*

Designer / *Maquettiste:* Linda Boyle

Publisher / *Éditeur:* Centaur Communications

ROTRAUT-SUSANNE BERNER

'Die Gespentsternacht'. Illustration for a Christmas book by Julien Green.
Coloured linocuts.

'Die Gespensternacht'. *Illustrations pour un livre de Noel par Julien Green.*
Linogravures colorées.

Designer / *Maquettiste:* Rotraut-Suzanne Berner

Publisher / *Éditeur:* Carl Hanser Verlag

ROTRAUT-SUSANNE BERNER

'Die Gespentsternacht'. Illustration for a Christmas book by Julien Green.
Coloured linocuts.

'Die Gespensternacht'. *Illustrations pour un livre de Noel par Julien Green.*
Linogravures colorées.

Designer / *Maquettiste:* Rotraut-Suzanne Berner

Publisher / *Éditeur:* Carl Hanser Verlag

IRENE GRANDADAM

" **'Troisième Tableau'** et **'Cinquième Tableau'** " . Theatre programme illustration for the play: 'La Vie Extraordinaire d'Antoine Riboud' by Rostropovitch .
Mixed media.

" *'Troisieme tableau'* et *'Cinquieme tableau'* " . *Illustration de programme pour la pièce de théâtre de Rostropovitch: 'La Vie Extraordinaire d'Antoine Riboud'.*
Techniques diverses.

Designer / *Maquettiste:* Marc Bruckert - Charles Petit

IRENE GRANDADAM

" **'Troisième Tableau'** et **'Cinquième Tableau'** ". Theatre programme illustration for the play: 'La Vie
Extraordinaire d'Antoine Riboud' by Rostropovitch .
Mixed media.

" *'Troisieme tableau'* et *'Cinquieme tableau'* ". *Illustrations de programme pour la pièce de théâtre de
Rostropovitch: 'La Vie Extraordinaire d'Antoine Riboud'.
Techniques diverses.*

Designer / *Maquettiste:* Marc Bruckert - Charles Petit

IRENE GRANDADAM

" 'Troisième Tableau' et **'Cinquième Tableau' ".** Theatre programme illustration for the play: 'La Vie Extraordinaire d'Antoine Riboud' by Rostropovitch .
Mixed media.

" 'Troisieme tableau' et *'Cinquieme tableau' ". Illustration de programme pour la pièce de théâtre de Rostropovitch: 'La Vie Extraordinaire d'Antoine Riboud'.
Techniques diverses.*

Designer / *Maquettiste:* Marc Bruckert - Charles Petit

JAN HISEK

Untitled. Illustration for a book by John Ronald Reuel Tolkien

Sans Titre. Illustration pour un livre de John Ronald Reuel Tolkien

LIONEL KOECHLIN

'Le réveillon du Père Noel'. Illustration for a book by Lionel Koechlin.
Acrylic.

*'Le réveillon du Père Noel'. Illustration pour un livre de Lionel Koechlin .
Acrylique.*

Designer / *Maquettiste:* Lionel Koechlin

Publisher / *Éditeur:* Hatier

LIONEL KOECHLIN

'Le réveillon du Père Noel'. Illustration for a book by Lionel Koechlin.
Acrylic.

'Le réveillon du Père Noel'. *Illustration pour un livre de Lionel Koechlin .*
Acrylique.

Designer / *Maquettiste:* Lionel Koechlin

Publisher / *Éditeur:* Hatier

VALERI VASILIEV

Illustration for a children's book by Maria Durechkova.
Oil paint.

Illustration tirées d'un livre d'enfants par Maria Durechkova.
Peinture à l'huile.

VALERI VASILIEV

Illustration for a children's book by Maria Durechkova.
Oil paint.

Illustration tirées d'un livre d'enfants par Maria Durechkova.
Peinture à l'huile.

VALERI VASILIEV

Illustration for a children's book by Maria Durechkova.
Oil paint.

Illustration tirées d'un livre d'enfants par Maria Durechkova.
Peinture à l'huile.

CAROLYN GOWDY

'Anne Frank, Diary of a Young Girl'. Illustration for a book.
Mixed media.

'Anne Frank, Diary of a Young Girl'. *Illustration pour un livre.*
Techniques diverses.

Designer / *Maquettiste:* Ian Butterworth

Publisher / *Éditeur:* Collins Publishers

PAVEL SIVKO

'Invisible Towns'. Illustration for a book by Italo Calvino.
Coloured pencil and chalk.

'Invisible Towns'. *illustration pour le livre de Italo Calvino*
Crayon de couleur et craie.

Designer / *Maquettiste:* Jan Jiskra

Publisher / *Éditeur:* Odeon

PAVEL SIVKO

'Invisible Towns'. Illustration for a book by Italo Calvino.
Coloured pencil and chalk.

*'Invisible Towns'. illustration pour le livre de Italo Calvino
Crayon de couleur et craie.*

Designer / *Maquettiste:* Jan Jiskra

Publisher / *Éditeur:* Odeon

PAVEL SIVKO

'Invisible Towns'. Illustration for a book by Italo Calvino.
Coloured pencil and chalk.

*'Invisible Towns'. illustration pour le livre de Italo Calvino
Crayon de couleur et craie.*

Designer / *Maquettiste:* Jan Jiskra

Publisher / *Éditeur:* Odeon

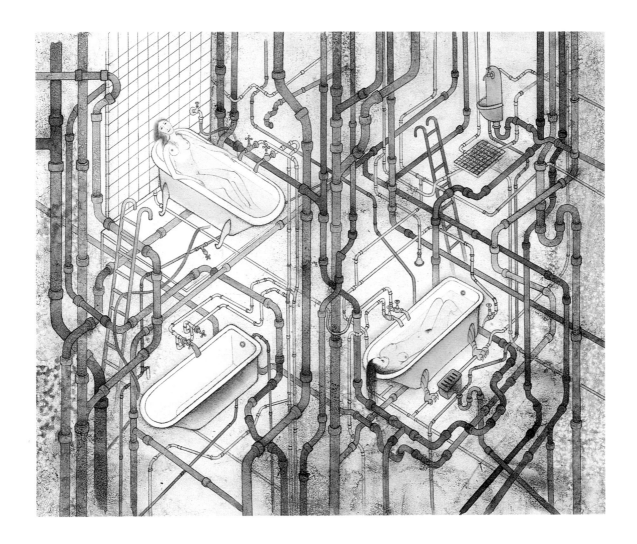

PAVEL SIVKO

'Invisible Towns'. Illustration for a book by Italo Calvino.
Coloured pencil and chalk.

'Invisible Towns'. illustration pour le livre de Italo Calvino
Crayon de couleur et craie.

Designer / *Maquettiste:* Jan Jiskra

Publisher / *Éditeur:* Odeon

GEOFFREY GRANDFIELD

'Intimacy'. Jacket illustration for a book by Susan Chase.
Chalk and pastel.

'Intimacy'. *Illustration de couverture pour un livre de Susan Chase.*
Craie et pastel.

Publisher / *Éditeur:* Serpents Tail

PETER KNOCK

'The Last Wednesday'. Jacket illustration for a book by Bernard Bannerman.
Watercolour.

'The Last Wednesday'. Illustration de couverture pour un livre de Bernard Bannerman.
Aquarelle.

Designer / *Maquettiste:* Peter Cotton

Publisher / *Éditeur:* Sphere Books Limited

CHRISTOPHER WORMELL

Illustration for an Alphabet Book by Christopher Wormell.
Linocut.

Illustration pour un Livre de l'Alphabet par Christopher Wormell.
Linogravure.

Designer / *Maquettiste:* Ian Butterworth

Publisher / *Éditeur:* Collins Children's Books

CHRISTOPHER WORMELL

Illustration for an Alphabet Book by Christopher Wormell.
Linocut

Illustration pour un livre de l'alphabet par Christopher Wormell.
Linogravure.

Designer / *Maquettiste:* Ian Butterworth

Publisher / *Éditeur:* Collins Children's Books

CHRISTOPHER WORMELL

Illustration for an Alphabet Book by Christopher Wormell.
Linocut.

Illustration pour un livre de l'alphabet par Christopher Wormell.
Linogravure.

Designer / *Maquettiste:* Ian Butterworth

Publisher / *Éditeur:* Collins Children's Books

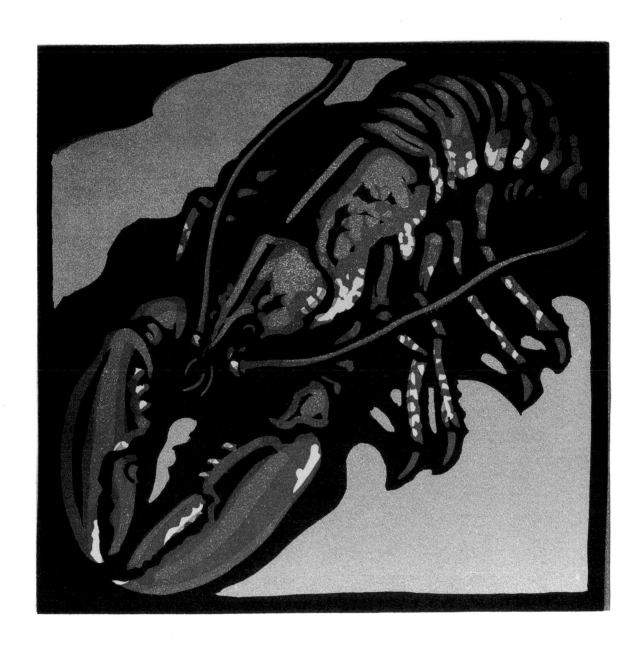

CHRISTOPHER WORMELL

Illustration for an Alphabet Book by Christopher Wormell.
Linocut.

Illustration pour un livre de l'alphabet par Christopher Wormell.
Linogravure.

Designer / *Maquettiste:* Ian Butterworth

Publisher / *Éditeur:* Collins Children's Books

IAN WHADCOCK

'The Use of Lateral Thinking'. Jacket illustration for a book by Edward De Bono.
Acrylic and varnish.

'The Use of Lateral Thinking'. *Illustration de couverture pour un livre d' Edward De Bono.*
Acrylique et vernis.

Designer / *Maquettiste:* Caz Hilderbrand

Publisher / *Éditeur:* Penguin Books

AXEL SCHEFFLER

'Daumesdich'. illustration for a book by Janosch.
Inks and colour pencils.

'Daumesdich'. illustration pour le livre de Janosch.
Encres et crayons de couleur.

Publisher / Éditeur: Hans-Joachim Gelberg

IAN POLLOCK

'Twentieth Century Suspense'. Jacket illustration for a book.
Ink.

'Twentieth Century Suspense'. Illustration de couverture pour un livre.
Encre.

Design Group / Agence de Design: Carroll, Dempsey & Thirkell

Publisher / *Éditeur:* The Macmillan Press Limited

KAREN LUDLOW

'World of Childrens' Books'. Cover illustration for a book by Michelle Landsberg.
Colour Linoprint.

'World of Childrens' Books'. *Illustration de couverture pour un livre de Michelle Landsberg.*
Linoprint couleur.

Designer / *Maquettiste:* Nick Pollitt

Publisher / *Éditeur:* Simon & Schuster

PAUL LEITH

'The Water Cat'. Jacket illustration for a book by Theresa Tomlinson.
Acrylic on paper.

'The Water Cat'. *Illustration de couverture pour un livre de Theresa Tomlinson.*
Acrylique sur papier.

Designer / *Maquettiste:* Ian Price and Jim Bunker

Publisher / *Éditeur:* Walker Books

PAUL LEITH

'The Encyclopedia of the Dead'. Jacket illustration for a book by Danilo Kis.
Acrylic on paper.

'The Encyclopedia of the Dead'. *Illustration de couverture pour un livre de Danilo Kis.*
Acrylique sur papier.

Designer / *Maquettiste:* John McConnell

Publisher / *Éditeur:* Faber + Faber

BORIS JIRKU

'Sto Roku Samoty'. Illustration for a book by G.H. Marquez.

'Sto Roku Samoty'. Illustration pour un livre de G.H. Marquez.

ANDRZEJ-LUDWIK WLOSZCZYNSKI

'**Hans Pfalff Adventure**'. Illustration for the Children's book, 'Moon's Road' by Maria Kann.
Ekoline and ink.

'***L'aventure de Hans Pfalff***'. *Illustration pour le livre d'enfants 'Moon's Road' de Maria Kann.*
Ekoline et encre.

Designer / *Maquettiste:* Andrzej-Ludwik Wloszczynski

Publisher / *Éditeur:* Kaw Wroclaw

JIRI SALAMOUN

'Die Hitze des Einfalls'. Illustration for a book by W. Heinse.
Pen and ink.

'Die Hitze des Einfalls'. Illustration pour un livre de W. Heinse.
Plume et encre.

Publisher / *Éditeur:* Eulenspiegel Verlag

JIRI SALAMOUN

'Die Hitze des Einfalls'. Illustration for a book by W. Heinse.
Pen and ink.

'Die Hitze des Einfalls'. *Illustration pour un livre de W. Heinse.*
Plume et encre.

Publisher / *Éditeur:* Eulenspiegel Verlag

JIRI SALAMOUN

'Pisne'. Illustration for a book by Jakub Jan Ryba.
Pen and ink.

'Pisne'. Illustration pour un livre de Jakub Jan Ryba.
Plume et encre.

JIRI SALAMOUN

'Pisne'. Illustration for a book by Jakub Jan Ryba.
Pen and ink.

'Pisne'. *Illustration pour un livre de Jakub Jan Ryba.*
Plume et encre.

JIRI SALAMOUN

'**Pisne**'. Illustrations for a book by Jakub Jan Ryba.
Pen and ink.

'**Pisne**'. *Illustrations pour un livre de Jakub Jan Ryba.*
Plume et encre.

JIRI SALAMOUN

'Tristram Shandy'. Illustrations for a book by Laurence Sterne.
Pen and Ink.

'Tristram Shandy'. *Illustrations pour un livre de Laurence Sterne.*
Plume et encre.

Publisher / Éditeur: Odeon

JIRI SALAMOUN

'Tristram Shandy'. Illustrations for a book by Laurence Sterne.
Pen and Ink.

'Tristram Shandy'. *Illustrations pour un livre de Laurence Sterne.*
Plume et encre.

Publisher / Éditeur: Odeon

JIRI SALAMOUN

'Tristram Shandy'. Illustrations for a book by Laurence Sterne.
Pen and Ink.

'Tristram Shandy'. *Illustrations pour un livre de Laurence Sterne.*
Plume et encre.

Publisher / Éditeur: Odeon

SIMEON SPIRIDONOV

Illustration for a book of Bulgarian Folk Tales.
Mixed media.

Illustration pour un livre de Comptes Populaires Bulgariens.
Techniques diverses.

Designer / *Maquettiste:* Simeon Spiridonov

Publisher / *Éditeur:* Otechestvo Publishing House

RICHARD PARENT

'The dark grave wherein my friend is laid'. Jacket illustration for a book by Malcolm Lowry.
Acrylic and oil pastel.

'The dark grave wherein my friend is laid'. *Illustration pour la couverture d'un livre de Malcolm Lowry.*
Acrylique et pastel à l'huile.

Designer / *Maquettiste:* Georges Sharp

Publisher / *Éditeur:* Pan Books

LOUISE BRIERLEY

'Nights at the Circus'. Jacket illustration for a book by Angela Carter.
Watercolour.

'Nights at the circus'. *illustration de couverture pour un livre de Angela Carter.*
Aquarelle.

Designer / *Maquettiste:* George Sharp

Publisher / *Éditeur:* Pan Books

LOUISE BRIERLEY

'The Fisherwoman'. Illustration for a book by Louise Brierley.
Watercolour.

'The Fisherwoman'. *Illustration pour un livre de Louise Brierley.*
Aquarelle.

Designer / *Maquettiste:* Sarah Hodder

Publisher / *Éditeur:* Walker Books

LOUISE BRIERLEY

'The Fisherwoman '. Illustration for a book by Louise Brierley.
Watercolour.

'The Fisherwoman '. Illustration pour un livre de Louise Brierley.
Aquarelle.

Designer / *Maquettiste:* Sarah Hodder

Publisher / *Éditeur:* Walker Books

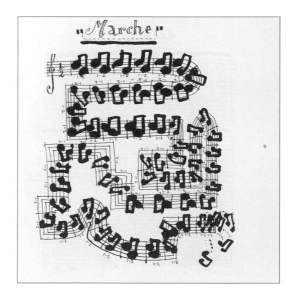

BENOIT JACQUES

'Play it by ear'. Illustrations for a promotional book by Benoît Jacques.
Pen and ink.

*'Play it by ear'. Illustrations pour un livre promotionnel de Benoît Jacques.
Plume et encre.*

Designer / *Maquettiste:* Benoît Jacques

Publisher / *Éditeur:* Benoît Jacques

133

BENOIT JACQUES

Illustrations for the Geers Gross Advertising agency twenty-fifth birthday book.
Watercolour, pen and ink.

Illustrations pour le livre du vingt-cinquième anniversaire de l'agence Geers Gross Advertising.
Aquarelle, plume et encre.

Designer / *Maquettiste:* Debbie Martindale

Publisher / *Éditeur:* Geers Gross Advertising Limited

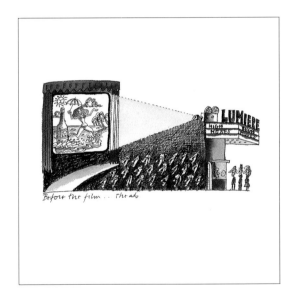

BENOIT JACQUES

Illustrations for the Geers Gross Advertising agency twenty-fifth birthday book.
Watercolour, pen and ink.

Illustrations pour le livre du vingt-cinquième anniversaire de l'agence Geers Gross Advertising.
Aquarelle, plume et encre.

Designer / *Maquettiste:* Debbie Martindale

Publisher / *Éditeur:* Geers Gross Advertising Limited

ADVERTISING

PUBLICITE

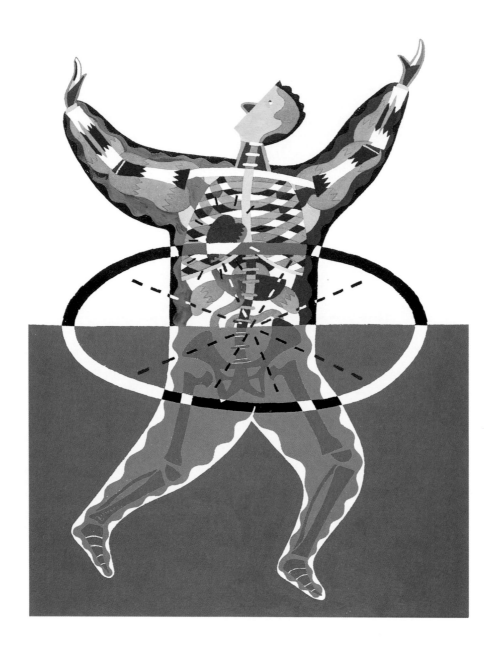

JEFF FISHER

'Medical Diagnosis'. Medical trade press advertisement.
Acrylic and watercolour.

'Diagnostic médical'. *Publicité de presse médicale.*
Acrylique et aquarelle.

Art Director / *Directeur artistique:* Ed Schriel/Frans Welter

Advertising Agency / *Agence de Publicité:* BVH Rotterdam

Client: Toshiba Medical Systems Europe

RONALD SLABBERS

'Gold colour coated Industrial parts'. International trade press advertisement.
Mixed media, coloured paper, thin thread and computer print out.

'Pièces Industrielles plaquées couleur or'. *Publicité de presse professionnelle internationale.*
Techniques diverses, papier couleur, fil fin, imprimerie par ordinateur.

Art Director / *Directeur artistique:* Hugo Van Bercum

Advertising Agency / *Agence de Publicité:* Riechelmann, Lopes Cardoza & Van Bercum

Client: Hauzer Techno Coating Europe B.V.

KATARINA JACOBSON

'Pork & Apple'. Promotional brochure illustration for 'Meat information'.
Mixed media.

'Porc et pomme'. *Illustration de brochure promotionnelle pour une information sur la viande.*
Techniques diverses.

Art Director / *Directeur artistique:* Henric Gustafson

Advertising Agency / *Agence de Publicité:* Gustafson & Haggblom

Client: Kottinformation - Swedish Meat Information

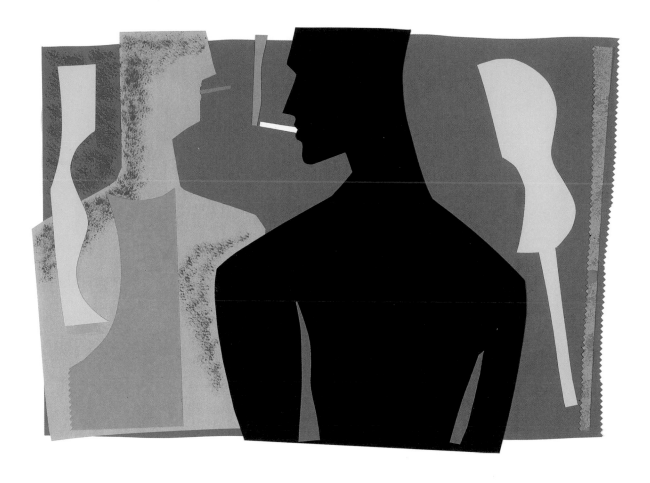

NICKY DUPAYS

'R1-R6 German Cigarettes'. Advertisement on T-shirt for a brand of cigarettes.
Cut paper and gouache.

'Cigarettes allemandes R1-R6'. *Publicité sur T-shirt pour une marque de cigarettes.*
Découpage et gouache.

Art Director / *Directeur artistique:* Christiane Herms-Glang / Erika Mademann

Advertising Agency / *Agence de Publicité:* Sholz + Friends

Client: Hf & Ph F-Reemtsma Gmbh & Lo

CHRISTOPHER WORMELL

Newspaper advertisement for a Dutch supermarket.
Wood engraving.

Publicité de presse pour un supermarché hollandais.
Gravure sur bois.

Art Director / *Directeur artistique:* Bela Stamenkovits

JEREMY SANCHA

Inheritance tax leaflet.
Linocut.

Plaquette sur la taxe d'héritage.
Linogravure.

Art Director / *Directeur artistique:* Bill Harrison

Advertising Agency / *Agence de Publicité:* Harcourt Design and Advertising

Client: Imperial Trident

BRIAN GRIMWOOD

'Medical equipment'. Medical trade press advertisement for a video endescopy.
Gouache.

'Equipement médical'. *Publicité de presse médicale pour une endescopie vidéo.*
Gouache.

Art Director / *Directeur artistique:* Ed Schriel / Frans Welter

Advertising Agency / *Agence de Publicité:* BVH Rotterdam

Client: Toshiba Medical Systems Europe

GARY POWELL

'Frank Lloyd Wright Furniture and Other Famous Designers'. Press advertisement.
Mixed media.

'Meubles de Frank Lloyd Wright et Autres Designers Célèbres'. Publicité de presse.
Techniques diverses.

Art Director / Directeur artistique: Robert Speechley / Neil French

Advertising Agency / Agence de Publicité: The Ball Partnership Singapore

Client: Diethelm Designer Furniture

POSTERS

AFFICHES

BRIAN CRONIN

'Don't waste water'. Self-promotion poster.
Pen, ink and overlay.

'Ne gaspillez pas l'eau'. *Affiche auto-promotionnelle.*
Plume, encre et film.

Art Director / *Directeur artistique:* Brian Cronin

Client: Brian Cronin

KAREN LUDLOW

Illustration for Ally Capellino summer fashion collection. Used as a poster.
Colour linoprint.

Illustration pour la collection de mode été de Ally Capellino. Utilisée pour un poster.
Linoprint couleur.

Art Director / *Directeur artistique:* Ally Capellino.

RICHARD PARENT

'L'annonce faite à Marie'. Theatre poster.
Acrylic, plus oil pastels.

'L'annonce faite à Marie'. *Affiche publicitaire pour une pièce de théâtre.*
Acrylique et pastels à l'huile .

Art Director / *Directeur artistique:* Richard Parent

Client: L'espace Go

Teatr Wielki im. Stanisława Moniuszki Poznań '88

GRZEGORZ MARSZALEK

'Giuseppe Verdi - Rigoletto'. Opera poster.
Acrylic and gouache

'Giuseppe Verdi - Rigoletto'. Affiche pour un opéra.
Acrylique et gouache

Art Director / *Directeur artistique:* Grzegorz Marszalek

Client: Poznan Opera

NICKY DUPAYS

'Shoerack'. Poster for a retail chain.
Cut paper and gouache.

'Shoerack'. *Affiche publicitaire pour une chaîne de boutiques.*
Découpage et gouache.

Art Director / *Directeur artistique:* Rebecca Fairman

Design Group / *Agence de Design:* Quadrangle Design Consultants

Client: Shoerack

NICKY DUPAYS

'Shoerack'. Poster for a retail chain.
Cut paper and gouache

'Shoerack'. *Affiche publicitaire pour une chaîne de boutiques.*
Découpage et gouache.

Art Director / *Directeur artistique:* Rebecca Fairman

Design Groupe / *Agence de Design:* Quadrangle Design Consultants

Client: Shoerack

LUCY COUSIN

'Easter Cards and Gifts'. Poster.
Gouache.

'Cartes de Pâques et Cadeaux'. *Affiche publicitaire.*
Gouache.

Art Director / *Directeur artistique:* Peter Kane

Advertising Agency / *Agence de Publicité:* Sears And Nalson

Client: W H Smith

NIKLAUS TROXLER

'Jagdszehnen'. Theatre poster.
Silkscreen.

'Jagdszehnen'. *Affiche pour une pièce de théâtre.*
Sérigraphie.

Art Director / *Directeur artistique:* Niklaus Troxler

Design Group / *Agence de Design:* Niklaus Troxler Grafik Studio

Client: Theatergesellschaft Willisan

ROBIN HARRIS

'Motorfair'. Poster for Motorfair 1989.
Acrylic.

'Motorfair'. *Affiche publicitaire pour le Salon de l'Automobile 1989.*
Acrylique.

Art Director / *Directeur artistique:* Paul Gay

Advertising Agency / *Agence de Publicité:* BMP DDB Needham

Client: Motorfair

ROLF JANSSON

Poster for the Norwegian railways.
Gouache.

Affiche publicitaire pour le chemin de fer Norvégien.
Gouache.

Art Director / *Directeur artistique:* Rolf Jansson

Client: Norwegian State Railways

BRIAN GRIMWOOD

Macallan art competition poster.
Gouache.

Affiche pour le concours artistique Macallan.
Gouache.

Advertising Agency / *Agence de Publicité:* Holmes Knight & Ritchie

Client: Macallan Whisky

RICHARD BEARDS

Christmas poster for a Design Group.
Gouache.

Affiche de Noël pour une Agence de Design.
Gouache.

Art Director / *Directeur artistique:* Robin Hall

Design Group / *Agence de Design:* Davies Hall

Client: Davies Hall

GRZEGORZ MARSZALEK

Exhibition poster.
Gouache.

Affiche d'exposition.
Gouache .

Art Director / *Directeur artistique:* Grzegorz Marszalek

Client: Bwa Art Exhibition Office

GRZEGORZ MARSZALEK

'James Joyce - The Wanderers'. Theatre poster.
Gouache

'James Joyce - Les Vagabonds'. Affiche pour une pièce de théâtre.
Gouache .

Art Director / *Directeur artistique:* Grzegorz Marszalek

Client: Stefan Jaracz Theatre

DESIGN

DESIGN

BILL SANDERSON

Illustration for Oban whisky label.
Scraperboard.

Illustration pour Oban whisky étiquette.
Carte à gratter.

Designer / *Maquettiste:* Mary Lewis

Art Director / *Directeur Artistique:* Mary Lewis

Design Group / *Agence de Design:* Lewis Moberly

LIZ PYLE

'Stirling Castle'. Cover illustration for Scottish Amicable report.
Pastel.

'Le Chateau de Stirling'. *Illustration de couverture pour un rapport de 'Scottish Amicable'.*
Pastel.

Designer / *Maquettiste:* Jenny Smith / Kenneth Craig

Art Director / *Directeur Artistique:* Jenny Smith

Design Group / *Agence de Design:* Graphic Partners Edinburgh

LIZ PYLE

'Bearing Fruit'. Cover illustration for Broughton Jacques self promotional brochure.
Pastel.

'Porter Fruit'. Illustration de couverture pour la brochure auto-promotionnelle de Broughton Jacques.
Pastel.

Designer / *Maquettiste:* David Bailey

Art Director / *Directeur artistique:* Gordon Jacques

Design Group / *Agence de Design:* Broughton Jacques Advertising Marketing Public Relations

JEFF FISHER

Illustration for the month of January in the 'Radio Diary 1990'.
Acrylic and watercolour.

Illustration pour le mois de janvier, dans l''Agenda Radio 1990'.
Acrylique et aquarelle.

Designer / *Maquettiste:* Julia Binfield

Art Director / *Directeur Artistique:* Julia Binfield

PAUL WEAR

Illustration   Diary 1990'.
Gouache

Illu   da Radio 1990'.
C

d

BILL DONOVAN

Illustration for the month of October in the 'Radio Diary 1990'.
Coloured paper.

Illustration pour le mois d'octobre dans l''Agenda Radio 1990'.
Papier coloré.

Designer / *Maquettiste:* Julia Binfield

Art Director / *Directeur Artistique:* Julia Binfield

STEVEN GUARNACCIA

Illustration for the 1991 year in the 'Radio Diary 1990'.
Marker and coloured pencil on brown paper.

Illustration pour l'année 1991, dans l' 'Agenda Radio 1990'.
Marker et crayon de couleur sur papier marron.

Designer / *Maquettiste:* Julia Binfield

Art Director / *Directeur Artistique:* Julia Binfield

WALTER VAN LOTRINGEN

'Man hopping over Q W E R T Y keys'. Support illustration for corporate brochure.
Computer generated image.

*'Un Homme sautant sur les touches Q W E R T Y'. Illustration support pour une plaquette institutionnelle.
Image conçue sur ordinateur.*

Designer / *Maquettiste:* Walter Van Lotringen

Art Director / *Directeur artistique:* Andre Toet

Design Group / *Agence de Design:* Samenwerkende Ontwerpers Amsterdam

WALTER VAN LOTRINGEN

'Man showing a burning lamp to another'. Illustration for corporate brochure.
Computer generated image.

'Un homme montrant une lampe brûlante à un autre'. *Illustration pour une plaquette institutionnelle.*
Image conçue sur ordinateur.

Designer / *Maquettiste:* Walter Van Lotringen

Art Director / *Directeur artistique:* André Toet

Design Group / *Agence de Design:* Samenwerkende Ontwerpers Amsterdam

WALTER VAN LOTRINGEN

'Post Office'. Illustration for Royal Mail calendar.
Ink and pastel.

__'La Poste'.__ Illustration pour le calendrier 'Royal Mail'.
Encre et pastel.

Designer / *Maquettiste:* Walter Van Lotringen

Art Director / *Directeur artistique:* Walter Van Lotringen

Design Group / *Agence de Design:* Dorland DFS

WALTER VAN LOTRINGEN

'Mailman wrapped in a roller coaster'. Illustration for Royal Mail calendar.
Ink and pastel.

'Un facteur enveloppé dans un grand huit'. *Illustration pour le calendrier Royal Mail.*
Encre et pastel.

Designer / *Maquettiste:* Walter Van Lotringen

Art Director / *Directeur artistique:* Walter Van Lotringen

Design Group / *Agence de Design:* Dorland DFS

ALISTAIR TAYLOR

Illustration for Northcroft corporate brochure.
Print.

Illustration de brochure institutionnelle pour Northcroft.
Print.

Designer / *Maquettiste:* Mervyn Kurlansky / Vanessa Ryan

Art Director / *Directeur Artistique:* Mervyn Kurlansky

Design Group / *Agence de Design:* Pentagram

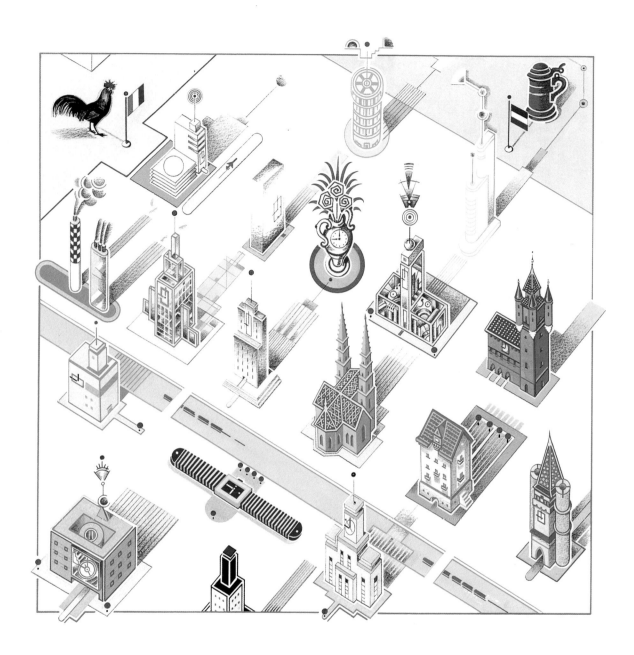

PETER BENTLEY

Brochure illustration promoting the 'Swiss Industrial Fair Centre'.
Ink, gouache and pencil.

Illustration pour une brochure promotant le 'Centre des Salons Industriels Suisses'.
Encre, gouache et crayon.

Designer / *Maquettiste:* Peter Bentley

Art Director / *Directeur Artistique:* Michael Schonhaus

HONKANEN HELMIRIITTA

'Exlibris'. Bus driver illustration.
P7/2 offset, two colours.

'Exlibris'. *Illustration pour conducteur de bus.*
P7/2 offset, deux couleurs.

Art Director / *Directeur Artistique:* Honkanen Helmiriitta

GUY BILLOUT

Annual report illustration for marine insurance company.
Mixed media.

Illustration pour un rapport annuel de compagnie d'assurance maritime.
Techniques diverses.

Designer / *Maquettiste:* Julie Fellowes

Art Director / *Directeur Artistique:* David Pearce

Design Group / *Agence de Design:* Tatham Pearce Limited

ROBIN HARRIS

Illustration for Touche Remnant UK Unit Trust brochure.
Acrylic.

Illustration pour la brochure 'UK Unit Trust' de la compagnie Touche Remnant.
Acrylique.

Art Director / *Directeur Artistique:* Judy Dalgleish of Touche Remnant

ANDREW KULMAN

'Ring Leaders'. Illustration for Telecom World Magazine.
Dry point and watercolour.

*'Les Anneaux Leaders'. Illustration pour 'Telecom World Magazine'.
Pointe sèche et aquarelle.*

Designers / Maquettistes: Lynn Trickett / Brian Webb / Avril Broadley

Design Group / *Agence de Design:* Trickett & Webb

BILL BUTCHER

'Managers should stand back from their business'. Illustration for ATZ Management Consultancy brochure.
Watercolour and gouache.

'Les managers devraient prendre du recul par rapport à leur business'. *Illustration pour la brochure
institutionnelle de ATZ Management Consultancy.
Aquarelle et gouache.*

Designer / *Maquettiste:* Mark Birch

Art Director / *Directeur Artistique:* Colin Robinson

Design Group / *Agence de Design:* Colin Robinson Associates Limited

ANNE HOWESON

Cover illustration for Touche Remnant report on their American Growth Fund.
Gouache.

Couverture de rapport pour le 'Fond de Croissance Americain' de la compagnie Touche Remnant.
Gouache.

Art Director / *Directeur Artistique:* Judy Dalgleish of Touche Remnant

JEFF FISHER

Illustration for IBM France brochure.
Ink, watercolour, acrylic.

Illustration pour la brochure IBM France.
Encre, aquarelle, acrylique.

Designer / *Maquettiste:* Colin Price

Art Director / *Directeur artistique:* Stuart Flanagan

Design Group / *Agence de Design:* Allan Cooper Associates

JEFF FISHER

Illustration for IBM France brochure.
Ink, watercolour and acrylic.

Illustration pour la brochure IBM France.
Encre, aquarelle et acrylique

Designer / *Maquettiste:* Colin Price

Art Director / *Directeur artistique:* Stuart Flanagan

Design Group / *Agence de Design:* Allan Cooper Associates

JEFF FISHER

Cover illustration for Star Typsetters type catalogue.
Acrylic.

Illustration de couverture pour le catalogue de caractères de la compagnie Star Typsetters.
Acrylique.

Designer / *Maquettiste:* Gez O'connell / Mark Watkins

Design Group / *Agence de Design:* Satellight

ANDREW KULMAN

One of a set of promotional posters issued by Buhrmann-Tetterode/RCA on the theme 'Graphic communications'.
Linocut, monoprint.

L'une des affiches promotionnelles issues par Buhrmann-Tetterode/RCA sur le thème 'Communications graphiques'.
Linogravure, monoprint on Japanese tissue.

Designer / *Maquettiste:* Andrew Kulman

Art Director / *Directeur Artistique:* Gerry Steijn

Design Group / *Agence de Design:* Top Drawers Amsterdam

CAROLYN GOWDY

'London has a problem, Mobira has the answer'. Cover illustration for the annual report
of a cellular telephone manufacturer.
Mixed media.

'Londres a un problème, Mobira a la réponse'. *Illustration de couverture pour le rapport
annuel d'un fabricant de téléphones cellulaires.
Techniques diverses.*

Designer / *Maquettiste:* Paul Carroll

Art Director / *Directeur Artistique:* Paul Carroll

Design Group / *Agence de Design:* Anderson Lembke

BENOIT JACQUES

'Laying recommendations'. Broadsheet cover illustration for a paving company.
Manual separation.

'Recommandations pour la pose'. *Illustration de couverture pour la plaquette format atlas
d'une compagnie de pavage.*
Separation manuelle.

Designer / *Maquettiste:* Benoît Jacques & Paul Anthony

Art Director / *Directeur Artistique:* Benoît Jacques

 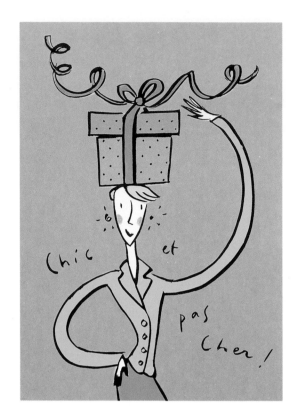

ISABELLE DERVAUX

Two of a series of sixty postcards published as a book.
Brush, ink and coloured pantone film

Deux cartes postales tirées d'une série de soixante autres publiées comme un livre.
Pinceau, encre et film pentone.

Designer / *Maquettiste:* Kenji Ishikawa

Art Director / *Directeur Artistique:* Tatsuomi Majima

Design Group / *Agence de Design:* Epic Sony Design Room

Publisher / *Éditeur:* Seiji Koseri

ISABELLE DERVAUX

Two of a series of sixty postcards published as a book.
Brush, ink and coloured pantone film.

Deux cartes postales tirées d'une série de soixante autres publiées comme un livre.
Pinceau, encre et film pentone.

Designer / *Maquettiste:* Kenji Ishikawa

Art Director / *Directeur Artistique:* Tatsuomi Majima

Design Group / *Agence de Design:* Epic Sony Design Room

Publisher / *Éditeur:* Seiji Koseri

ISABELLE DERVAUX

Two of a series of sixty postcards published as a book.
Brush, ink and coloured pantone film.

Deux cartes postales tirées d'une série de soixante autres publiées comme un livre.
Pinceau, encre et film pentone.

Designer / *Maquettiste:* Kenji Ishikawa

Art Director / *Directeur Artistique:* Tatsuomi Majima

Design Group / *Agence de Design:* Epic Sony Design Room

Publisher / *Éditeur:* Seiji Koseri

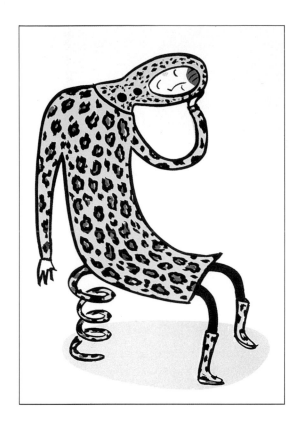 

ISABELLE DERVAUX

Two of a series of sixty postcards published as a book.
Brush, ink and coloured pantone film.

Deux cartes postales tirées d'une série de soixante autres publiées comme un livre.
Pinceau, encre et film pentone.

Designer / *Maquettiste:* Kenji Ishikawa

Art Director / *Directeur Artistique:* Tatsuomi Majima

Design Group / *Agence de Design:* Epic Sony Design Room

Publisher / *Éditeur:* Seiji Koseri

ISABELLE DERVAUX

Two of a series of sixty postcards published as a book.
Brush, ink and coloured pantone film.

Deux cartes postales tirées d'une série de soixante autres publiées comme un livre.
Pinceau, encre et film pentone.

Designer / *Maquettiste:* Kenji Ishikawa

Art Director / *Directeur Artistique:* Tatsuomi Majima

Design Group / *Agence de Design:* Epic Sony Design Room

Publisher / *Éditeur:* Seiji Koseri

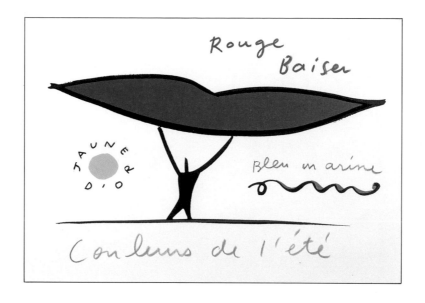

ISABELLE DERVAUX

Two of a series of sixty postcards published as a book.
Brush, ink and coloured pantone film.

Deux cartes postales tirées d'une série de soixante autres publiées comme un livre.
Pinceau, encre et film pentone.

Designer / *Maquettiste:* Kenji Ishikawa

Art Director / *Directeur Artistique:* Tatsuomi Majima

Design Group / *Agence de Design:* Epic Sony Design Room

Publisher / *Éditeur:* Seiji Koseri

ISABELLE DERVAUX

Packaging for a new range of Cookies.
Brush and ink with amberlith overlays.

Emballage pour une nouvelle variété de Cookies.
Encre et pinceau avec films d'ambre.

Art Director / *Directeur artistique:* Isabelle Dervaux

ISABELLE DERVAUX

Packaging for a new range of Cookies.
Brush and ink with amberlith overlays.

Emballage pour une nouvelle variété de Cookies.
Encre, pinceau et films d'ambre.

Art Director / *Directeur artistique:* Isabelle Dervaux

CLIFFORD HARPER

Calendar illustration.
Screen print.

Illustration de calendrier.
Sérigraphie.

Designers / Maquettistes: Lynn Trickett / Brian Webb / Avril Broadley

Design Group / *Agence de Design:* Trickett & Webb

PIERRE LE TAN

Calendar illustration.
Screen print.

Illustration de calendrier.
Sérigraphie.

Designers / Maquettistes: Lynn Trickett / Brian Webb / Avril Broadley

Design Group / *Agence de Design:* Trickett & Webb

ANDREW KULMAN

Calendar illustration.
Screen print.

Illustration de calendrier.
Sérigraphie.

Designers / Maquettistes: Lynn Trickett / Brian Webb / Avril Broadley

Design Group / *Agence de Design:* Trickett & Webb

JEFF FISHER

Calendar illustration.
Screen print.

Illustration de calendrier.
Sérigraphie.

Designers / Maquettistes: Lynn Trickett / Brian Webb / Avril Broadley

Design Group / *Agence de Design:* Trickett & Webb

PHILIPPE WEISBECKER

Calendar illustration.
Screen print.

Illustration de calendrier.
Sérigraphie.

Designers / Maquettistes: Lynn Trickett / Brian Webb / Avril Broadley

Design Group / *Agence de Design:* Trickett & Webb

ANIMATION

ANIMATION

ULI MEYER

'Traffic Warden'. Animation.

'Contractuelle'. Animation.

Art Director / *Directeur Artistique:* Pascal Hierholz

Director / *Réalisateur:* Pete Bishop

Production Company / *Compagnie de Production:* The Film Garage

Client: Mars Chocolate.

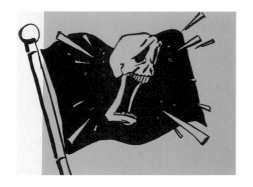
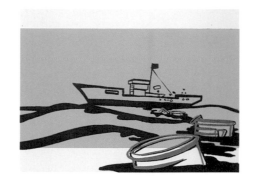
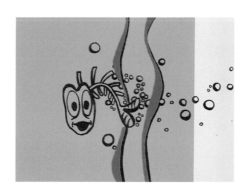

DAVE COCKBURN JONATHON BAIRSTOW DAVE BURGESS DINO ATHANASSIOU RAVI SWAMI.

'Not my Problem'. Animation.

'Pas mon problème'. Animation.

Art Director / *Directeur Artistique:* Marc Kitchen-Smith

Director / *Réalisateur:* Marc Kitchen-Smith

Production Company / *Compagnie de Production:* The Film Garage

Client: MTV Europe

UNPUBLISHED
PROFESSIONAL

*PROFESSIONNELS
NON PUBLIES*

GEOFFREY GRANDFIELD

One from a series of sixteen pictures for an audio-visual presentation of 'The Tramp Woman's Tragedy', by Thomas Hardy. Commisioned but not used.
Chalk pastel.

Illustration tirée d'une série de seize images pour une présentation audio-visuelle de 'The Tramp Woman's Tragedy', par Thomas Hardi. Commandée, non utilisée.
Craie pastel.

Design Group / *Agence de Design:* Topaz Production

GEOFFREY GRANDFIELD

One from a series of sixteen pictures for an audio-visual presentation of 'The Tramp Woman's Tragedy', by Thomas Hardy. Commisioned but not used.
Chalk pastel.

Illustration tirée d'une série de seize images pour une présentation audio-visuelle de 'The Tramp Woman's Tragedy', par Thomas Hardi. Commandée, non utilisée.
Craie pastel.

Design Group / *Agence de Design:* Topaz Production

ANDREW MOCKETT

'The Man who saved clouds'. Two key frames from a commercial for the Bank of Scotland.
Commissionned but not used.
Pastel.

'L'homme qui sauva les nuages'. *Deux images clefs, tirées d'un film commercial pour Bank of Scotland.*
Commandées, non utilisées.
Pastel.

Art Director / *Directeur Artistique:* Mark Reddy

ANDREW MOCKETT

'**The Man who saved clouds**'. Two key frames from a commercial for the Bank of Scotland.
Commissionned but not used.
Pastel.

'***L'homme qui sauva les nuages***'. *Deux images clefs, tirées d'un film commercial pour Bank of Scotland.*
Commandées, non utilisées.
Pastel.

Art Director / *Directeur Artistique:* Mark Reddy

BENOIT JACQUES

'Conversation'. Personal project.
Acrylic on paper.

'Conversation'. *Projet personnel.*
Acrylique sur papier.

BENOIT JACQUES

'Man and Dog'. Personal project.
Acrylic on paper.

'Homme et Chien'. *Projet personnel.*
Acrylique sur papier

GARY MICHAEL EMBURY

'Johnny the Kid'. Personal project.
Watercolour, gouache and pencil

'Johnny le Gamin'. *Projet personnel.*
Aquarelle, gouache et crayon.

GARY MICHAEL EMBURY

'Denizen'. Personal project.
Watercolour, gouache and pencil.

'Denizen'. Projet personnel.
Aquarelle, gouache et crayon.

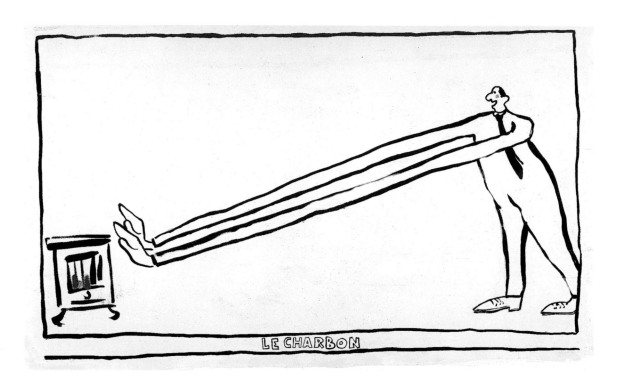

GIOVANNI GUARINI

'Le charbon'. Promotional poster for coal. Commissioned by 'Promoteur du Charbon', but not used.
Acrylic.

'Le charbon'. *Affiche publicitaire pour la promotion du charbon. Commandée par 'Promoteur du Charbon', non utilisée.*
Acrylique.

Art director / *Directeur Artistique:* Giovanni Guarini

DOVRAT BEN-NAHUM

Press ads for EL-AL Airlines. Commissioned but not used.
Watercolour, gouache and pencil.

Publicité de presse pour EL-AL Airlines. Commandée non utilisée.
Aquarelle, gouache, crayon.

Art Director / *Directeur Artistique:* Yosep Ohayon

Design Group / *Agence de Design:* Kesher Barel

GARIF BASYROV

'**Man in sea**'. Personal project.

'**Homme à la mer**'. *Projet personnel.*

GARIF BASYROV

'Landscape'. Personal project.

'Paysage'. Projet personnel.

CLARE JARRETT

'Stress'. Illustration commissionned for New Woman Magazine, but not used.
Print.

'Stress'. *Illustration commandée pour le magazine 'New Woman', non utilisée.*
Print.

Designer / *Maquettiste:* Sue Miller

JIM FIEDING

'The Wood Cutter'. Personal project.
Mixed media.

'Le bucheron'. *Projet personnel.*
Techniques diverses.

GRETTA KOOL

Untitled.
Photomontage.

Sans titre.
Photomontage.

JENNIFER BENT

'Josie feeding the Puppies'. Illustration from 'My Caribbean Home'. Commissioned by
Beanstalk Books but not used.
Ink on watercolour paper.

'Josie nourrit les petits'. Illustration pour le livre ' Ma Maison des Caraïbes'. Commandée par
Beanstalk Books, non utilisée.
Encre sur papier aquarelle.

PETER SUTTON

'Urban Landscape'. Unpublished.
Acrylic.

'Paysage Urbain'. *Non publié.*
Acrylique.

CHRIS PRIESTLEY

'Taksim Square'. Portfolio illustration.
Acrylic.

'Taksim Square'. *Illustration pour portfolio.*
Acrylique.

MICHAEL O'SHAUGHNESSY

'The Tea Drinkers'. Personal project.
Watercolour and chalk.

'Les buveurs de thé'. *Projet personnel.*
Aquarelle et craie.

STUDENT

ETUDIANTS

MIKEY GEORGESON

'**The Golden Bird**'. Illustration for student portfolio.
Linocut, monoprint.

'*L'oiseau doré*'. *Illustration pour portfolio d'étudiant.*
Linogravure, monoprint.

MIKEY GEORGESON

'The Goose Girl'. Illustration for student portfolio.
Linocut, monoprint.

'La Guardienne d'oies'. *Illustration pour portfolio d'étudiant.*
Linogravure, monoprint.

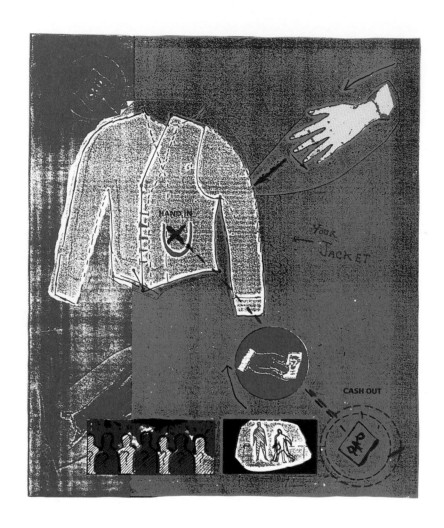

ANDREW BAKER

'The Pickpockets' Perfect Plan'. One of four illustrations for portfolio: 'Five ways to lose your money'.
Offset litho.

'Le plan parfait des pickpockets'. *Tirée d'une série de quatre illustrations pour portfolio:*
'Five ways to lose your money'.
Litho offset.

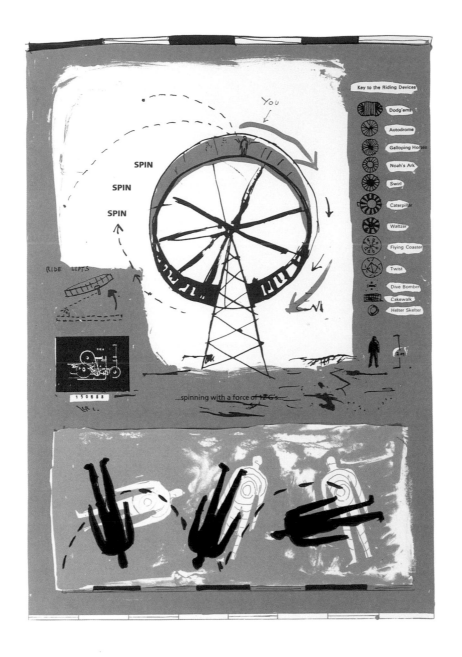

ANDREW BAKER

'The Big Wheel of Gravity'. One of four illustrations for portfolio: 'Five ways to lose your money'.
Offset litho.

'La grande roue de la gravité'. Tirée d'une série de quatre illustrations pour portfolio:
'Five ways to lose your money'.
Litho offset.

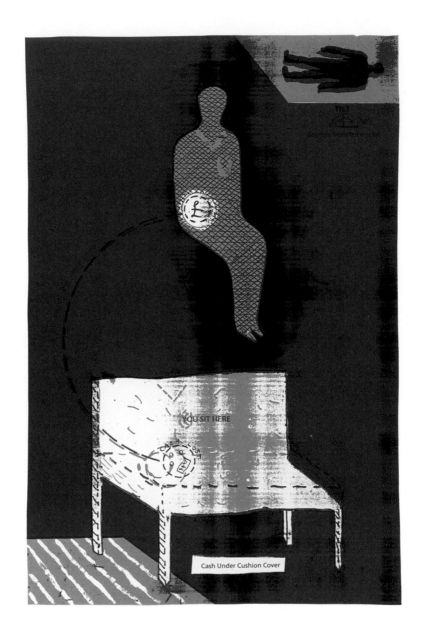

ANDREW BAKER

'Cash under cushion cover'. One of four illustrations for portfolio: 'Five ways to lose your money'.
Offset litho.

'Cash sous l'enveloppe du coussin'. *tirée d'une série de quatre illustrations pour portfolio*
'Five ways to lose your money'.
Litho offset.

ANDREW BAKER

'A hole in my pocket'. One of four illustrations for portfolio: 'Five ways to lose your money'.
Offset litho.

'Un trou dans ma poche'. *Tirée d'une série de quatre illustrations pour portfolio: 'Five ways to lose your money'.*
Litho offset.

ANDREW BAKER

'Mugged by a Masked Marauder'. Postcard from the portfolio: 'Five ways to lose your money'.
Colour xerox and collage

'Agressé par un marauder masqué'. *Carte postale tirée du portfolio: 'Five ways to lose your money'.*
Xerox couleur et collage.

NICK BARKER

'Diner - Long Island'. Illustration from a series of paintings during a trip to the United States.
Oil paint on cardboards and wood.

*__'Diner - Long Island'.__ Illustration tirée d'une série de peintures realisées lors d'un voyage aux Etats-Unis.
Peinture à l' huile sur carton et bois.*

JOANNA PARRY

'Design History in Schools: what your art teacher never taught you'. Illustration for an article in
a college magazine.
Pencil crayon.

*'L'Histoire du Design à l'école: ce que votre professeur d'art ne vous a jamais enseigné'. Illustration pour un
article dans un magazine de collège.*
Crayon.

ROBERT ALLEN

'The conformist'. Illustration for student portfolio.
Acrylic on tissue paper.

'Le conformiste'. *Illustration pour portfolio d'étudiant.*
Acrylique sur papier de soie.

LYDIA EVANS

Cover illustration for Shostakovich Symphony N 8 compact disc. Student portfolio.
Coloured tissue paper (collage), ink and bleach.

Illustration de couverture pour un disque compact de Shostakovich: Symphonie N 8. Portfolio d'étudiante.
Papier de soie coloré (collage), encre et décolorant.

INDEX

INDEX

AKIB, JAMEL
14 Cliffsea Grove
Leigh-on-Sea
Essex

ALLEN, ROBERT
c\o European Illustration
12 Carlton House Terrace
London SW1Y 5AH

ATHANASSIOU, DINO
The Film Garage
143 Wardour Street
London W1

BAIRSTOW, JOHNATHON
The Film Garage
143 Wardour Street
London W1

BAKER, ANDREW
67a Kentish Town Road
London
NW1 8NY

BARKER, NICK
1 Saint Johns Road
Ansley Common Nuneaton
Warwickshire

BASYROV, GARIF
Matveyevskaya ul Pen
Kor 2 KV 354
Moscow 119517

BEARDS, RICHARD
19 Arundel Gardens
London
W11 2LN

BEN-NAHUM, DOVRAT
83 Canfield Gardens
London
NW6 3EA

BENT, JENNIFER
142 Queens Road
Watford Herts
WD1 2NX

BENTLEY, PETER
c\o CIA
36 Wellington Street
London WC2

BERNARD, PIERRE-NOEL
2 Rue de la Republique
42000 Saint-Etienne
France

BERNER, ROTRAUT-SUSANNE
Ziegelhauser Landstrasse 31
D-6900 Heidelberg
West Germany

BILLOUT, GUY
225 Lafayette Street
Room 1008 New York
NY 1002 USA

BLOMMESTIJN, RHONALD
Artbox
Kruislaan 182-1098
SK-Amsterdam Holland

BOUVIER, STANISLAS
c\o Le Village
68 Rue Joseph de Maistre
75018 Paris France

BRIERLEY, LOUISE
65 Highbury New Park
London
N5 2ET

BRIERS, STUART
33 Eswyn Road
London
SW17 8TR

BURGESS, DAVE
The Film Garage
143 Wardour Street
London W1

BUTCHER, BILL
24 Kidbrooke Park Road
London
SE3 0LW

BYLO, ANDREW
38b Southwell Road
London
SE5 9PG

COCKBURN, DAVID
The Film Garage
143 Wardour Street
London W1

COUSINS, LUCY
29 Windsor Road
Petersfield
Hampshire

CRONIN, BRIAN
8 Terenure Park
Terenure
Dublin 6W Ireland

DENVIR, CATHERINE
1 Saint Andrews Road
London
W14 9SX

DERVAUX, ISABELLE
c\o Philippe Arnaud Agent
184 Rue de l'Universite
74007 Paris France

DONOVAN, BILL
7 East 14th Street
New York
NY 10003 USA

DRUMMOND, ALLAN
c\o The Artworks
75 Filmer Road
London SW6 5BJ

DUDZINSKI, ANDRZEJ
54 East 81 Street
New York
NY 10028 USA

DUPAYS, NICKY
c\o European Illustration
12 Carlton House Terrace
London SW1Y 5AH

EMBURY, GARY
The Inkshed
54-58 Tanner Street
London SE1 3PH

EVANS, LYDIA
90 Windermere Avenue
Hullbridge
Essex SS5 6JT

FIELDING, JIM
26 Netley House
Southampton Way
London SE5 7EY

FISHER, JEFF
c/o C.I.A.
36 Wellington Street
London WC2

GAMMAGE, CHUCK
The Film Garage
143 Wardour Street
London W1

GEORGESON, MIKEY
45 Stafford Road
Brighton
Sussex BN1 5PE

GOLDMAN, BART
344 West 23rd Street
6B New York
NY 10011 USA

GOWDY, CAROLYN
2c Maynard Close
Off Cambria Street
London SW6 2EN

GRANDADAM, IRENE
18 Rue Micolon
94140 Alfortville
France

GRANDFIELD, GEOFFREY
c\o Folio
10 Gate Street
London WC2

GRIMWOOD, BRIAN
c/o CIA
36 Wellington Street
London WC2

GRUNDY, PETER
Thames Wharf Studio
Rainville Road
London W6

GUARINI, GIOVANNI
c/o Dupont
67 Rue du Bailli
1050 Bruxelles Belgium

GUARNACCIA, STEVEN
430 West 14 Street - 508
New York
NY 10014 USA

HARPER, CLIFFORD
78a Crofton Road
London
SE5 8NA

HARRIS, ROBIN
60 Weltje Road
London
W6 9LT

HELMIRIITTA, HONKANEN
Vehaksentie 14
02300 Espoo
Finland

HISEK, JAN
Barrandovska 16
150 00 Praha
Czechoslovakia

HOLROYD, HELEN
36 Bernard Road
Brighton
Sussex BN2 3EQ

HOWESON, ANNE
91 Cloudesley Road
London
NN1 0EL

HUGHES, DAVID
Rosemount Studios
43 Station Road
Marple Cheshire SK6 6AJ

JARRETT, CLARE
54 Clarendon Road
Norwich
NR2 2PW

JACOBSON, KATARINA
Vasterled 43
16137 Bromma
Sweden

JACQUES, BENOIT
95 Hanover Road
London
NW10 3DL

JANSSON, ROLF
Radyrstien 44
3190 Horten
Norway

JIRKU, BORIS
Rooseveltova 24
Praha 6
16000 Czechoslovakia

KNAFF, JEAN-CHRISTIAN
c\o Folio
10 Gate Street
London WC2

KNOCK, PETER
17 Nelson Drive
Leigh on Sea
Essex SS9 1DA

KOECHLIN, LIONEL
18 Avenue Mozart
75016 Paris
France

KOOL, GRETTA
45 Westbourne Terrace
London
W2

KULMAN, ANDREW
Basement Flat
1 Jenner Rd
London N16 7SB

LE TAN, PIERRE
4 Rue Saint Augustin
75002 Paris
France

LEITH, PAUL
37 Therapia Road
London
SE22 OSF

LUDLOW, KAREN
c\o Sharp Practice
Unit 30 Waterside
44-48 Wharf Road London N1

MARSZALEK, GRZEGORZ
Os. Kosmonautow 20/72
61-642 Poznan
Poland

MOCKETT, ANDREW
Flat 4
118 Marine Parade
Brighton BN2 1DA

MORRIS, JOHN
Folio
10 Gate Street
London WC2

MORRISON, TOBY
45 Easterbury Grove
London
W4

MUNOZ, CLAUDIO
c/o European Illustration
12 Carlton House Terrace
London SW1Y 5AH

NASCIMBENE, YAN
78 Rue des Archives
75003 Paris
France

NICKLIN, RAY
26 Alma Road
Penylan
Cardiff CF2 5BD

NORTON, JEREMY
Fab 4 Studio
60 Arley Hill
Bristol BS6 5PP

O'SHAUGHNESSY, MICHAEL
c\o The Organisation
69 Caledonian Road
London N1 9BT

OSTROWSKA, ANNA
Nijverheidstr 3
3071 GA
Rotterdam Holland

PARENT, RICHARD
c\o Sharp Practice
Unit 30 Waterside
44-48 Wharf Road London N1

PARRY, JOANNE
33 Christopher Crescent
Poole
Dorset BH15 3HQ

PAVKO, SIVKO
Na Baste Sv.Ludmily 17/245
16000 Prague
Czechoslovakia

PIGLIA, PAOLA
28 Cliff Street
3 New York
NY 10038 USA

POLLOCK, IAN
Flat C
34 Anson Road
London N7 OAB

POWELL, GARY
c/o Sharp Practice
Unit 30 Waterside
44-48 Wharf Road London N1

PRIESTLEY, CHRIS
45 Charlotte Road
London
EC2A 3PD

PYLE, LIZ
94 Ravenscroft Street
London
E2 7QA

SALAMOUN, JIRI
Parizska 10
11000 Prague
Czechoslovakia

SANCHA, JEREMY
23 Beck Road
London
E8 4RE

SANDERSON, BILL
Fernleigh
Huntingdon Road Houghton
Cambridgeshire PE17 2AU

SCHEFFLER, AXEL
30 Telford Avenue
London
SW2 4XF

SHEEHY, MICHAEL
Flat 2
89 Choumert Road
London SE15 4AP

SLABBERS, RONALD
Plantage Parklaan 11
1018 St Amsterdam
Holland

SLATER, PAUL
22 Partridge Close
Chesham
Bucks HP5 3LH

SOBR, PENELOPE
Flat 4
149 Holland Park Avenue
London W11 4UX

SPIRIDONOV, SIMEON
OKR Perniski
2430 Dren
Bulgaria

SUTTON, PETER
8 Saint Johns Path
Hitchin
Herts SG4 9DA

SWAMI, RAVI
The Film Garage
143 Wardour Street
London W1

TAYLOR, ALISTAIR
The Inkshed
54-58 Tanner Street
London SE1 3PH

TILL, PETER
7 Queensgate Villas
Victoria Park Road
London E9

TROXLER, NIKLAUS
Postfach CH 6130
Willisau
Switzerland

VAN LOTRINGEN, WALTER
Nic Maesstr 132
1071 RH
Amsterdam Holland

VASILIEV, VALERI
Saintankevicha Street 16/4 '52
Moscow 108009
USSR

WEARING, PAUL
3 Leigh Street
London
WC1 H9EW

WEBSTER, DAVID
30 Melbourne Avenue
London
W13 9BT

WEISBECKER, PHILIPPE
136 Waverly Place
New York
NY 10014 USA

WHADCOCK, IAN
38 Stanford Avenue
Brighton
Sussex BN1 6EA

WOOLLEY, JANET
34 Stanhope Road
London
N6 5N6

WORMELL, CHRIS
The Artworks
75 Filmer Road
London SW6

WTOSZCZYNSKI, ANDRZEJ
Foksal 17m57
00372 Warsaw
Poland

YOUNG, ALAN
2 Chapel Cottages
Dunks Green Tonbridge
Kent TN11 9SF

THE EUROPEAN ILLUSTRATION COLLECTION IN HULL ILLUSTRATORS AND ARTISTS

These are the illustrators and artists who have had work accepted in European Illustration since it started in 1973. Their work is eligible to be in the European Illustration Collection.

LA COLLECTION D'ILLUSTRATIONS EUROPEENES A HULL ILLUSTRATEURS ET ARTISTES

Ceux-ci sont les illustrateurs et artistes dont le travail a été accepté dans European Illustration depuis le début en 1973. Leur travail est éligible pour figurer dans la Collection d'Illustrations Europeennes.

Abdellah, Stephen
Abrahams, Bob
Albus, Anita
Adams, Richard
Adams, Stephen
Adams, Tom
Adler, Alan
Adsett, Gillian
Akib, Jamel
Alcantarilla, Susan
Alcorn, John
Aldduck, Don
Aldridge, Alan
Allen, Julian
Allen, Paul
Allin, John
Almansa, Severo
Aloof, Andrew
Alterio, Caroline
Amadieu, Francoise
Ambro, Hal
Ames, Nicola
Anderson, Wayne
Andreassen, Alf-Magne
Andrews, Gary
Andus, Hilary
Anelli, Liz
Angel, Debi
Apicella
Appleby, Steven
Appleton, Geoffrey
Areopage
Arisman, Marshall
Assenat, Jean Marie
Audras, Agnes
Audus, Hilary
Avallone, Gennaro

Babs
Bachelet, Gilles
Badmin, Sydney
Bagdaschwilli, Wasyl
Baileul, Claude
Baird, Vanessa
Bairstow, Jonathan
Baker, Alan
Baker, Andrew
Baker, Barry
Baldwin, Richard
Ball, Sarah
Ballesta, Juan
Baran, Zafer
Barber, Norman
Barbosa, Arthur
Bardsley, Chris
Barnett Henry
Barraclough, Ian

Barrett, Peter
Barrow, Christine
Barsacq, Alberte
Bass, Saul
Basyrov, Caroline
Batten, Karin
Bauer, John
Baur, Gilles Marie
Baxter, David
Bayley, Nicola
Beard, Pete
Beards, Richard
Beasley, Olivia
Beck, Ian
Beeke, Anthon
Belina, Renate
Belingradt, Wolfgang
Belletty, Ray
Benee, Derek
Bennallack, Hart M. J.
Bennet, Madeleine
Bennion, Michael
Bentley, Peter
Bents, Nigel
Ben-Nahum, Dovrat
Bergentz, Torsten
Berner Rotraut, Susanne
Berthoin, Christine
Besson, Jean Louis
Bijl, Liz
Bijlsma, Ronald
Billebeau, Jacques
Billout, Guy
Binch, Carol
Binfield, Julia
Birbeck, Paul
Bird, Malcolm
Bishop, Pete
Blagden, Robert
Blake, Peter
Blake, Quentin
Blatch, Bernard
Blum, Gunter
Blume, Karin
Blumrich, Christof
Bodek, Stuart
Bordignon, Mirella
Bonen, Keith
Bonhomme, Bernard
Born, Adolf
Borowski, Pedda
Botero, Fernando
Botti, Rene
Boucher, Joelle
Bouille, Pierre
Bour, Daniele
Bourne, Roger

Box, Leonora
Boxer, Marc
Boyd, Harte Glynn
Bracken, Paula
Bradley, Gill
Braids, Braldt
Brauchli, Pierre
Brenders, Carl
Bretecher, Claire
Brett, Bob
Brett, David
Brett, Wendy
Breughel, Pieter
Briant, Edward
Bridges, Ned
Brierley, Louise
Briers, Stuart
Briggs, Raymond
Brimage, Christina
Bristow, Sara
Brookes, Peter
Brooks, Tom
Broutin, Christian
Brown, Christopher
Brown, Ken
Brownfield, Mick
Bru, Salvador
Bruce, Nichola
Brusch, Beat
Brusilorsky, A.
Bryant, David
Buckingham, Lesley
Buj, Roman
Bull, David
Butcher, Bill
Butt, Bill
Bylo, Andrew

Calder, Emma
Calderley, David
Caley, Patricia
Campbell, Alastair
Canosa, Pier
Caron, Philippe
Carr, Pauline
Carruthers, Roy
Cartwright, Reg
Caselli, Giovanni
Castle, Philip
Cattolica, Hector
Cauquil, Olivier
Chalmer, Fred
Chapman, Leslie
Chatterton, Martin
Chauvin, Henri
Cheese, Chloe
Chesterman, Adrian

Chichester-Clarke, Emma
Chwast, Seymour
Clark, John
Clark, Peter
Clarke, Graham
Claveloux, Nicole
Clayden, Alwyn
Clement, Marina
Clifton-Dey, Richard
Cober, Alan
Cockcroft, Dave
Coe, Sue
Coffinieres, Herve
Coker, Peter
Cole, Lo
Coleman, Roger
Collicott, Chris
Collins, Terry
Comte, Michel
Comte, Robert
Condula, Max
Cony, Frances
Cook, Debbie
Cook, Micky
Cook, Peter
Coombs, Roy
Coplans, Peta
Coppenhall, David
Corentin, Philippe
Corke, Boogie
Cornuel, Pierre
Corr, Christopher
Cosford, Bob
Costantini, Flavio
Coulson, Mike
Countakis, Sofocles
Couratin, Patrick
Cox, Ken
Cox, Patrick
Cox, Paul
Cracknell, Alan
Craddock, Barry
Craft, Kinuko
Craker, Brian
Cramer, Jon
Crane, Mick
Cremer, Jan
Crocker, Lee
Cronin, Brian
Crowther, Robert
Cruz, Jose
Cuadrado, Heriberto
Culver, Murdo
Cummins, Jeff
Curless, Alan
Curtis, Susan
Cutter, David

Hirtler, Christof
Hockney, David
Hodanson, Lars
Hodgson, Jonathan
Hofmann, Godi
Hofmann, Marie
Hofmann, Werner
Hogarth, Paul
Hoier, Heiner
Hoile, Wendy
Holderness, Griselda
Hollis, Kaarl
Hollyhead, Bush
Holmes, David
Holmes, Diana
Holmes, John
Holmes, Nigel
Hood, Alun
Hook, Bob
Hortelano, El
Houles, Pierre
Houston, Jannat
Howard, John
Howeson, Anne
Huber, Jorg
Huggins, David
Hughes, David
Huller, Manus
Huntley, Sue
Hurford, John
Hutton, Peter

Ibbett, Vera
Innocenti, Roberto
Ireland, John

Jackson, David
Jackson, Jeff
Jacques, Benoit
Jacques, Faith
James, Brian
Jan, Daniel
Jarrett, Clare
Jeker, Werner
Jelliffe, Ray
Jenkins, Danny
John, Sarah
Johnson, Michael
Jones, Allan
Jones, Chris
Jones, Helen
Jonsson, Dan
Jordaan, Peter
Joyner, Jerry
Juniper, David
Kaiser, R. I.
Kalasat, Loris

Kanters, Hans
Kee, Rory
Keleck
Kelley, Peter
Kemeny, Gyorgy
Kemp, Moira
Kettle, Peter
Kieffer, Carol
Kirby, Ron
Kitchen-Smith, Marc
Klemm, Traudy
Klonaris, Laurence
Knaff, Jean-Christian
Knight, Brian
Knight, Laura
Knipe, Royston
Knipe, Roy
Knock, Peter
Kochl, Edda
Koechlin, Lionel
Koether, M.
Koscielniak, Cyprian
Krauze, Andrzej
Krawczyk, Sabine
Kroese, Yvonne
Kubrick, Dana
Kulman, Andrew
Kunkel, H. P.
Kunz, Anita
Kyte, Ray

Labayle, Sophie
Lacroix, J.
Lagarrigue, Jean
Laidlaw, Ken
Laing, Sandy
Lakich, Lili
Lambie-Nairn, Martin
Lamotiniere, Pascal
Lampert, Pete
Landis, Urs
Langer-Rosa, Marina
Langford, Frank
Lap, Wouter
Lapointe, Claude
Larkin, Simon
Larriere, Jean Jacques
Larue, Patrice
Launder, Sally
Lawrence, Jo
Lawrie, Bob
Le Saux, Alain
Le Vasseur, Peter
Learmonth, Larry
Leconte, Michel
Lee, Adrian
Lee, Alan

Lefoll, Alain
Leith, Paul
Leman, Martin
Lemoine, Georges
Leonard, Michael
Leonard, Tony
Leray, Alain
Lessenich, Jean
Lettick, Birney
Levitow, Ave
Lewis, Garth
Lewis, Richard
Le-Tan, Perre
Lichthardt, Ulrich
Liddell, Tom
Liegent, Olivier
Lilly, Kenneth
Lincoln, Philip
Lindholm, Anders
Lindley, Katrin
Litherland, Mike
Litter, Ernst
Llewellyn, Sue
Lockwood, Gaye
Lodge, Bernard
Loeb, Catherine
Lofthouse, Barbara
Lomax, Peter Gordon
Lopez, Antonio
Loppe, Michel
Lord, Peter
Loris, M.
Lovell, Andrew
Luck & Flaw
Lucques
Lumbers, Clive
Lunt, Michael
Lutton, Jean Claude
Lyonnet, Jean Pierre

Maas, Harro
Mac, John
MacAllister, Patrick
Mackay, Neil Adam
Mackenzie, Muriel
Mackinnon, Steward
Mactavish, Euphemia
Macvicar, Fiona
Maddison, Kevin
Mader, Gerlinde
Madill, Warren
Magenta, Studios
Maggioni, Federico
Magill, Anne
Mairs, Nigel
Majera, Helene
Malish, Miro

Manham, Allan
Manning, Richard
Marsh, Graham
Marsh, James
Marszalek, Grzegorz
Martin, Pauline
Martin, Gillian
Martinez, Gadea Vicente
Martinez, Mina
Mason, Robert
Matchavariani, Henri
Matthews, Tony
Mau, Michael
Maza, Fernando
McCall, Iain
Mcdonald, Joyce
McDonald, Neil
McElmurray, Gill
McEwan, Chris
McEwan, Keith
McGowan, Shane
McGrail, Rollin
McInnery, Micke
McIntosh, Roger
McLean, Wilson
McManus, Hilary
McMenemy, Sarah
McMillan, Sean
McMullan, Jeames
McNab, Andrew
McNaughton, Colin
McSweeney, Tony
Meeuwissen, Tony
Megenta, Studios
Meisel, Ann
Melander, Lars
Melinsky, Claire
Merat, Guy
Mercer, Ron
Merre, Maupeou
Messi, Enzo
Meuse, Angus
Meyer, Michel
Midda, Sara
Mihaesco, Eugene
Milas, Pino
Millet, Roland
Mills, Russell
Minichello, Mario
Miranda, Santiago
Mitchell, Glen
Mitscka, Will
Mleckzo, Andrzej
Mlodozeniec, Jan
Mockett, Andrew
Monson-Baumgart, Isolde
Moore, Anthony

Moore, Chris
Moore, Norman
Moo-Young, Ian
Morchoisne, Claude
Morrillon
Morrow, Anne
Morter, Peter
Muir, Donna
Mulatier, Jean
Mulazzani, Giovannia
Muman, Mariet
Munoz, Claudio
Murawski, Alex
Murdoch, Bob
Murray, Karen
Murray, Roger
Musnier, Yves
Mynott, Gerald
Mynott, Lawrence

Nadler, Ellis
Nanson, Steve
Nascimbene, Yan
Navarres
Newman, Colin
Nicholas, George
Nix, Robert
Noome, Mike
Norrington, Bob
Northedge, Tilly
North, Peter
Numan, Mariet
Nystrom, Bengt

Odello, Maximillien
Ogden, Ray
Oppermann, Wolfgang
O.P.S.
Orr, Richard
Osmond, Lucinda
Osterlin, Anders
Osterwalder, Ulrich
Osti, Maurizio
Ostrowska, Anna
Owen, Peter
Oxenbury, Helen
Oxenham, Patrick
O'Brien, Kevin
O'Brien, Teresa
O'Higgins, David
O'Neil, Andy
O'Riordan, Barry
O'Shaughnessy, Michael

Page, Nick
Pages, Francoise
Paisley, Pam
Palayer, Jean

Palfrey-Rogers, Graham
Palmer, David
Parent, Richard
Parker, Beverley
Parnel, Jacques
Pascalini, Gabriel
Pastor, Terry
Patterson, Neil
Paul, Charlie
Pearce, David
Pearce, Jack
Pearce, Robert
Pearson, Matthew
Penney, David
Percy, Graham
Perramon, Jean Maxim
Perret, Paul
Peters, Hilke
Petit, Chantal
Peyrolle, Pierre
Pfeiffer, Walter
Pickard, Cynthia
Pickard, Steven
Pierre, Sophie
Piglia, Paola
Pimentel, Antonio
Pinn, Ingram
Piper, Christian
Piper, Tom
Pizzoti, Laurent
Plaquin, Philippe
Platt, Gillian
Platt, Theo
Pocknell, David
Polasz, Monica
Police, Lou
Pollock, Ian
Poncet de la Grave
Ponnighaus, M. P.
Potter, Ashley
Potter, Nick
Powell, Gary
Preston, Alan
Preston, Gerry
Price, Nick
Prosser, Bill
Pudles, Daniel
Pugh, Anna
Purdum, Richard
Pyle, Liz

Q.E.D.
Quarez, Michel
Quay Brothers, The
Rabanelly, Michel
Raby, Michel

Randall, Tony
Ranken, Josephine
Rauch, Hans George
Rawle, Graham
Raymond, Charles
Rayne, Paul
Redgrave, Paul
Rees, Alan
Rehill, Chris
Reinhard, Dietmar
Reiser, Willi
Remo, Berselli
Renard, Jean Marie
Renault, Jean Michel
Richardson, Peter
Ricord, Patrice
Riding, Lynne
Rieckhoff, Jan
Riediger, Henning
Rinciari, Ken
Ringger, Art
Roben, Paul
Robert, Jean Edouard
Roberts, Mary
Robins, Arthur
Robins, Christine
Rockwood, Richard
Roelofsz, Joost
Rose, John
Rosenbaum, Sarah
Rosenberg, Kristin
Rosenthal, M.
Roskilly, Peregrine
Ross, Michelle
Ross, Tony
Rosy, Maurice
Rottke, Helmut
Rousset, Francoise
Roux, Guillelmo
Rowlands, Wil
Rowney, Mark
Rozenberg, Marcel
Rozier
Rush, Ken
Russell, George
Russo, Anthony
Ryder, Johanne

Salmon, Neil
Sample, Paul
Sancha, Jeremy
Sanders, Brian
Sanderson, Bill
Sannicolo, G.
Sanseau
Santos, Jocelyn
Sardet, Claude
Sawyer, David

Scarfe, Gerald
Scharpf, Manfred
Scheffler, Axel
Schenfield, Richard
Schlohmann, Renate
Schossow, Peter
Schroeder, Binnette
Schudel, Anne Marie
Schultz, Monica
Schwartzman, Arnold
Searle, Ronald
Seelow, Manfried
Selden, Roger
Selig, Sylvie
Sequin, Ken
Sendall, Morgan
Shannon, Faith
Sharp, Anne
Sharp, George
Sharratt, Nick
Sharrock, Christopher
Shepherd, Mark
Shuster, Nigel
Sidwell, Anthony
Siedlecka, Barbara
Simard, Yves
Simeon, Michel
Simmonds, Posy
Simonetti, Sergio
Simpson, Christine
Sio, Enrico
Skogberg, Gerrard
Slabbers, Ronald
Slater, Paul
Slocombe, Romain
Smart, Kevin
Smax, Willy
Smee, Andrew
Smidt, Urs
Smith, Anne
Smith, Caroline
Smith, Janet
Smith, Ken
Smith, Trevor
Snow, George
Sobr, Penelope
Sorel, Edward
Soyka, Ed
Spiegelmann, Art
Spiro, Lorraine
Spohr, Heinz
Sproxton, David
Stanczyk, Grzegorz
Stanton, Jane
Steadman, Ralph
Steen, Birgitta
Stepan, Bohumil

Stephenson, Mike
Stern, Simon
Stolk, Swip
Stoneham, Marion
Strater, Volker
Strugnell, Anne
Stuart, Michael
Stubberfield, Mary
Stymest, Brian
Suter, David
Suyling, Karel
Swan, Peter

Taback, Simms
Taggart, Nick
Tait, Don
Tamba, Harry
Tardi, Jacques
Tattersfield, Brian
Taylor, Alastair
Taylor, Tom
Tee, Francis
Teja, Ramon Gonzales
Tenney, Eric
Terry, Mike
Theimer, Ivan
Thijssen, Andre
Thirsk, John
Thomas, Mark
Thompson, Graham
Thompson-Steinkrauss, J.
Thorne, Jenny
Thos, Graham
Thos, Yves
Thumer, Guenther
Tibbles, Jean-Paul
Till, Peter
Tipton, Claire
Titus
Toner, Michael
Topor, Roland
Toral, Christobal
Tosetto, Jacques
Traeger, Tessa
Trengove, Barry
Trevithick, Michael
Tribe, John
Tripp, Jan Peter
Tromp, Erno
Trouche, Claude
Troxler, Niklaus

Underwood, George
Ungerer, Tomi
Unwin, David
Vaka Guire, Michel
Valenti, Celestino

Valentine, Jim
van Anderson, Kjell
van Den Berg, Arja
van der Jagt, Martin
van der Poll, Bas
van Gelder, Kees
van Groningen, Suze
van Leeuven, Bart
van Lotringen, Walter
van Raalte, Rene
Vanemden, Ans
Varieras, Claude
Varlet, Pierre
Vassiliev, Cyril
Veistola, Jukka
Verberk, John
Vester, Paul
Vieweg, Cecil
Vinton, Will
Voce, Louise
Vogel, Manfred

Waechter, Friedrich Karl
Wallis, Diz
Wallis, Rolland
Walter, Dorothee
Wandrey, Peter
Wane, Pete
Warwickshire Illustrators
Watson, Donald
Wearing, Paul
Weaver, Norman
Webb, Paul
Webb, Povl
Weever, Peter
Wefers, Dietmar
Wells, Tony
Welponer, Karin
Wenner, Tom
Werner, Jeker
Wetter, Beatrix
White, Charles
White, Martin
White, Tony
Whitlock, Lily
Widmann, Joachim
Wiedemann, Kay
Wiese, Bruno K.
Wiesmuller, Dieter
Wigren, Christina
Wilcox, David
Wilhelmsen, Hildur Kristin
Wilkinson, John
Williams, Kit
Williams, Richard
Willock, Harry
Wilson, Bob

Wilson, Chrissy
Wilson, Franklin
Wilson, John
Wilson, Roland
Winder, Ray
Winterbotham, Ann
Wisenfeld, Alison
Witt, Rolf
Wolstenholme, Jonathon
Wood, Owen
Wood, Sidney
Woodruff, Thomas
Woolley, Janet
Woolmer, Chris
Woolston, Geoff
Wormell, Christopher
Worth, David
Wright, Freire
Wright, Joseph
Wright, Tony
Wurr, Matthew
Wyatt, Kathy
Wyss, Peter

Yamamoto, Sato
Young, Ed
Young, Susan
Zagorski, Stanislaw
Zanoni, Murray
Ziegenfeuter, Dieter
Zlatkovski, Michail
Zoladz, Stanislaw